Practical Management Methods

An Accountable Approach to Managing Others

The Leader's Heart

Allow me to get a bit philosophical for just a moment. I believe that management is a high calling. Management is a serious responsibility—not just to the company but also to the manager's fellow employees and those who have invested in the company. I know that it never feels that way when new managers are in their first supervisory role. New managers are frequently doing all that they can just to keep their heads above water among all of the unforeseen challenges they begin to encounter.

When we are allowed to step into that first job as a manager or supervisor, the excitement and pride associated with achieving the position is sometimes dissipated quickly. Once employees feel comfortable enough with the new boss they will learn what "buttons" to push and when. Just like young children pushing the limits of their parents' patience, they will probe to find weaknesses in the leader before a negative reaction is generated. Expect it, because it will happen.

Management is a lot like parenting. Being a parent demands a number of skills that are not necessarily instinctive to every human being. Among these are being a good listener; being able to exercise extreme patience; and being supportive when necessary balanced against those times when strict discipline is required. Parenting requires that the children be given room to try new things even if they don't always work out for the best.

Management is exactly the same. As managers we must demonstrate patience at the same time that we are pushing for deadlines. Managers must be able to listen (sometimes more than they speak) and understand when employees are testing them versus when they really need help. Managers must be able to tolerate mistakes (and what they cost in time and treasure) if employees are to grow. Management is parenting.

If you don't have children, take heart. You are not doomed to failure because of this. You will need to reach back in your memories to try to reflect on how your own parents saw things as you were growing up. The resulting fresh perspective will improve your skills and increase your appreciation for what Moms and Dads go through.

Beyond Philosophy

Many leaders wrestle with "connecting the dots" between their professional journey and their faith walk. Our society's embrace of human diversity and strident application of the constitutional separation of church and state makes us think twice before turning to faith as a source for leadership insights. In fact, it often seems as though the requirements of business leadership and the teachings of Jesus Christ are mutually exclusive, but they're not.

The Answers Have Been There All Along

The best leadership guide ever written is also the single most popular book in all of human history – the Holy Bible. Using dramatic retellings that depict both the good and the evils of leadership, the Old Testament contains the full spectrum of human emotions within its pages – love, hate, greed, generosity, triumph and tragedy, to name but a few. The New Testament includes instructions for living based on the teachings of Jesus Christ. Christ used parables and specific directions to establish His (and God's) expectations of us. Our success or failure as a leader depends, in large measure, on how completely we are able to practice the principles of grace, compassion and respect that Jesus taught us; but is reciting Scripture at your next management team meeting the most effective means of honoring the Great Commission?

Non-Christians need not be reluctant to identify with the guidelines for living contained in the New Testament. People of different faiths have adopted the behaviors and attitudes espoused by Jesus, without violating the teachings of their own faith. They succeed because these characteristics define a "universal" commission to treat one another with grace, compassion and basic human respect. Could there be anything more relevant to the practice of leadership?

Start At the Beginning

Any discussion of management techniques must begin with an understanding of the true role of a manager. There are many different definitions of "manager," based largely on "who" is doing the defining. A popular dictionary defines "manager" in this way:

> MANAGER: One who handles, controls, or directs, especially: a. one who directs a business or other enterprise. b. One who controls resources and expenditures, as of a household. 2. One who is in charge of the business affairs of an entertainer. 3. Sports a. One who is in charge of the training and performance of an athlete or a team. b. A student who is in charge of the equipment and records of a school or college team.[1]

As with many English language words, the definition varies based upon context. For our purposes we are only concerned with definition #1 – "One who handles, controls, or directs..." This is the context in which we must function. Our daily tasks are a combination of handling, controlling and directing people, processes and resources. In addition to these tasks, however, are a large number of other responsibilities seldom mentioned in any dictionary. The table below presents a number of unusual roles that I think are an integral part of being a manager in an organizational setting. At one time or another during your management career you will feel like you must play all of these roles (and in some cases be expected to). Being a manager is so much more than just being in charge and carries with it a heavy burden of accountability for those things which cannot truly be controlled.

- Counselor
- Parent
- Prophet
- Spiritual Advisor
- Psychologist
- School Administrator
- Friend
- Teacher
- Buddy
- Mentor

- Dictator
- Leader

An Alternative Definition

Most dictionaries would not include the list above in their definitions of manager and management. So I propose the following multi-part alternative concept of managing.

Perhaps the single most important capability for any manager is having the ability to exert influence without the stimulus of intimidation. Being able to influence others to behave in a particular manner or perform some task you need them to perform is the keystone of successfully managing your team. I believe that the best definition of "manager" is dramatically different from the dictionary version referenced above.

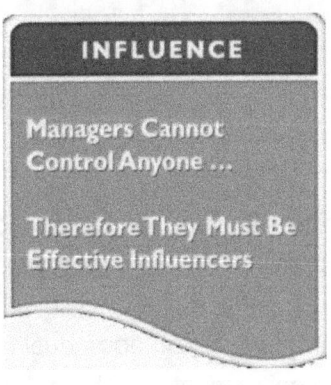

INFLUENCE

Managers Cannot Control Anyone ...

Therefore They Must Be Effective Influencers

BEHAVIORS

Managers Must Get Others to Behave in Ways They Normally Would Not

So what should influence be used for? Managers must motivate their team to perform tasks that they might otherwise not do on their own. For example, a foreman in a steel plant must ask the steelworkers to put themselves into a work environment that is dangerous, uncomfortable and stressful. Would anyone not so motivated eagerly take this on? Perhaps not.

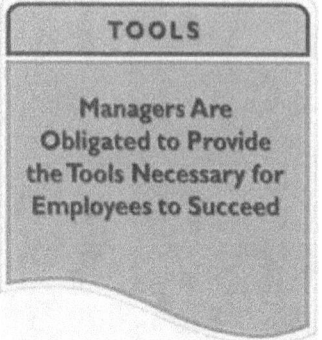

TOOLS

Managers Are Obligated to Provide the Tools Necessary for Employees to Succeed

Managers are accountable for providing their team whatever tools are necessary to complete the mission at hand. The manager need not be clairvoyant – staff members must let the manager know when they need something not already provided. Tools can include anything from actual hand tools to software to more staff. The form is immaterial; the obligation is absolute.

This is critical: Expectations must be correctly set for employees so that they can adopt the sense of urgency or intolerance of poor quality (or both) of management. There must be clear objectives documented and made available to employees, from which decisions can be made about accomplishing the work. Failure by managers in this area can result in significant project failures.

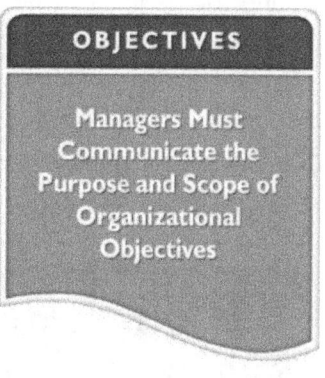

OBJECTIVES

Managers Must Communicate the Purpose and Scope of Organizational Objectives

LATITUDE

Managers Need to Grant Employees the Latitude to Learn From Their Mistakes

Managers must give their team the latitude to do the job, without constant monitoring and correcting (aka micromanaging). It makes sense though, especially if the manager has done the previous items well. When mistakes are made, managers must respond appropriately, but if at all possible allow the misstep to be a teaching moment rather than remembered for punishment.

Notice that there is absolutely nothing in this definition about being in charge, being the boss, making up the rules, etc. Such "control" statements are characteristics of a job description, not of a manager. Managers who are unable to recognize the need to achieve their team or company objectives through effective influencing of associates and subordinates will fail.

Leadership versus Management

Noted management guru Peter Drucker is often credited with stating that "Management is do things right; leadership is doing the right things." The subtle yet profound distinction this statement suggests is often lost on new managers. Much has been written to explain the differences between managers and leaders, but the kernel of the matter is that managers deal everyday with what "is" while leaders try to spend each day working to define what "will be."

Managers are frequently said to be transactional and leaders transformational. The skills required of successful managers are not necessarily the same skills required of effective leaders. Warren Bennis is a noted author of leadership resources and distinguished business professor at the University of Southern California. Bennis argues that "There is a profound difference between management and leadership and both are important. To manage means to bring about, to accomplish, to have charge of or responsibility for, and to conduct. Leading is influencing, guiding in a direction, course, action, opinion. The distinction is crucial.

Bennis has developed a comparative guide for understanding the distinctions between leaders and managers.[2]

- The manager administers; the leader innovates.
- The manager maintains; the leader develops.
- The manager accepts reality; the leader investigates it.
- The manager focuses on systems and structures; the leader focuses on people.
- The manager relies on control; the leader inspires trust.

- The manager has a short-range view; the leader has a long-range perspective.
- The manager asks how and when; the leader asks what and why.
- The manager has his or her eye always on the bottom line; the leader has his or her eye on the horizon.
- The manager imitates; the leader originates.
- The manager accepts the status quo; the leader challenges it.
- The manager is the classic good soldier; the leader is his or her own person.

So, it would seem, that leadership is about being visionary—being able to see beyond the here and now to what might be coming next, whether speaking about products, trends, resources or, perhaps most importantly, people. In contrast, management is about knowing what can be achieved with the products, resources and people available at hand.

This is no insignificant or trivial difference. Every organization, regardless of size, focus or longevity, desperately needs both strong managers and strong leaders. Both skill sets are infrequently found in one person. That is why managers and leaders are often thought of as a "team", because it takes more than one to play the game. Managers and leaders are critical assets of any organization—public, private or non-profit—and they must be viewed with distinction.

From your own experience, think about examples of people who were great leaders or great managers (or both). Why they were admired within their respective roles and which character traits or practices you would most like to emulate?

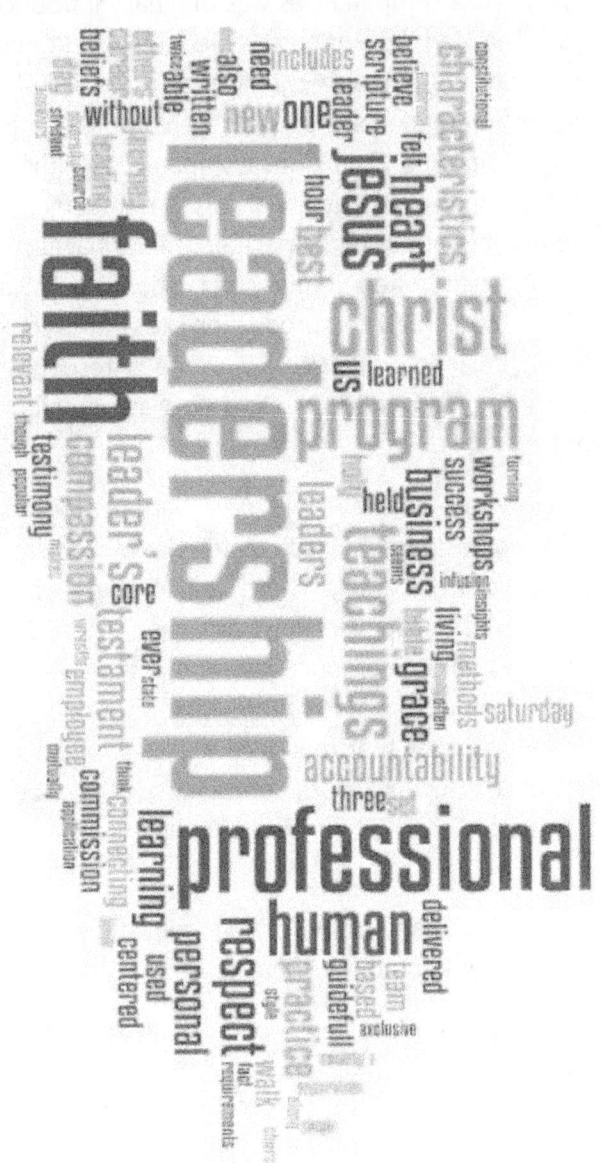

Core Passions & Competencies

The concept of core competencies was originally introduced in 1990 in an article for The Harvard Business Review by C.K. Prahalad and Gary Hamel. Prahalad, a distinguished university professor of management and Hamel, an international management consultant, collaborated to produce an article titled "The Core Competence of the Corporation." They contended that it was essential for corporations to look at their competitiveness, but not from the perspective of what each business unit in the company has to offer. Rather corporation need to examine what the collective technological and production skills of the company are and how they can best be organized to create a responsive, adaptable organization. The following is a straightforward description of a core competency:

> "A core competency can take various forms, including technical/subject matter know how, a reliable process and/or close relationships with customers and suppliers (Mascarenhas et al. 1998). It may also include product development or culture such as employee dedication. Modern business theories suggest that most activities that are not part of a company's core competency should be outsourced."[3]

According to Prahalad and Hamel, a core competency of a corporation must display the following three characteristics:

- The competency provides potential access to a wide variety of markets.
- The competency increases perceived customer benefits.
- The competency is hard for competitors to imitate.

Many management theory experts and scientists have expanded on the work of Prahalad and Hamel, adapting their original treatise to advance their own notions, including how core competencies apply at an individual as well as corporate level. This has been invaluable for the practice of management because it has helped to frame the discussion in such a way that it makes it practical for the vast majority of business managers who wish to develop their own skills to study the concepts.

If you think about the core competencies of an entire business as if it were matter in the marketplace universe, then you might also think of core competencies for individuals as the atomic particles that form the matter. While corporate core competencies are viewed as an aggregate reflection of the competitiveness and sustainability of the company, individual core competencies necessarily reflect the passions, distinctive talents, skills and capabilities of the people who make up the teams which function inside a corporation. It is critically important for these competencies to be cataloged as part of a strategic and vibrant management model. For example, it does no good for a business to decide to manufacture and sell toasters if no one in the company knows anything about bread. While the example is, admittedly, overly simplistic, the truism it represents is not: Businesses must consider what their collective organic skills enable them to successfully undertake in order to be competitive, adaptive and sustainable.

The Passions & Core Competencies of a Manager

Just as individual workers have distinct core competencies that make them unique, specific job functions within an organization have characteristics (or competencies) that are necessary in order for the person performing in that job to be successful. For instance, talented carpenters have many innate skills, such as fundamental engineering instinct, strong spatial conceptual aptitude and an artistic creativity that understands intuitively how different textures and colors blend together into a whole. Such people may find enjoyment working in the remodeling business or building fine furniture. Yet such capabilities would not necessarily be the right ones necessary to fill a position as a production manager in a modular home manufacturing facility. Why? Because understanding carpentry is not the primary competency required to successfully manage a production project as complex as an entire modular home. (There are plumbing and electrical specifications that are equally critical to the finished product but which do not qualify these subject matter experts to take the senior production job either.)

A better fit for the production manager's role would be someone who has a broad-based background that includes some level of knowledge of the carpentry, electrical and plumbing fields, as well as

- someone who understands how to create a reliable estimate for completing work
- someone with experience in developing schedules for the acquisition and deployment of resources (both human and material)
- someone who has successfully led work teams under time driven deadlines
- someone who can be equally comfortable talking with customers as they are with fellow craftsman

The fundamental rule of thumb is this: Subject matter experts in a particular field do not necessarily have the requisite skills, aptitude, attitude, demeanor, patience, etc., to lead a team of subject matter experts in the same field.

Being a manager is a demanding job that is unlike anything that non-managers have ever conceived of. Many newly appointed managers have been shocked to learn that being the "manager" has a lot less to do with being "in charge" than they expected. Management is a complex mosaic of skills and instincts that must be applied to accomplishing some concept or unit of work. A manager must possess all of the components of the mosaic, albeit in varying volumes or levels, in order to truly be successful (and, generally, happy). What follows is a sampling of the core competencies managers should be able to count among their own:

- Strong "people" orientation
- Insight into human behavior patterns

- Effective communication skills
- Commitment to excellence
- Patience and high tolerance for mistakes
- High stress tolerance
- Rigorous honesty
- Unflinching ethics
- Ability to perform simple mathematics quickly
- Intermediate skills with office productivity software

Nowhere in that list will you find a reference to a specific industry, product or service. Such specialized knowledge is helpful to be sure, desirable if possible but not always required. Two high-profile appointments of CEOs are great examples where industry expertise was not required. Ford Motor Company hired Alan Mulally as CEO to succeed Bill Ford. Mulally was serving as CEO of Boeing Commercial Airplane Group when Ford tapped him to lead the struggling automaker. Mulally had no previous experience running a major auto manufacturer, yet the Board of Directors at Ford felt that his knowledge of what it takes to build a commercial airplane—one of the most complex systems ever devised by man—would be a good basis for helping them to improve their overall performance.

Equally incompatible (or so it would seem) was the decision by the new owners of Chrysler to appoint Robert Nardelli as CEO. Nardelli had been CEO of Home Depot for seven years prior to joining Chrysler. Again, any obvious linkages between home repair retailing and automotive manufacturing are nearly impossible to cite. (In fact, Nardelli had no retailing experience when he joined Home Depot from his senior position at General Electric.) What Nardelli did possess was a set of core competencies in total quality management and organizational leadership that helped Home Depot to nearly double its sales and profits during Nardelli's tenure. Chrysler, as the troubled junior member of the American "Big Three" car makers, likely felt it needs the core competencies that Nardelli brings to the table.

So, you may ask, why should I care? Consider these observations:

- We don't manage machines – we manage people
- Clock-punchers have a role, but it's generally not at the management table
- Employee morale is increasingly difficult to steer
- Everyone wants more of a smaller pie (and believes they're entitled to it)
- We need to have the right people doing the right job
- Dedicated, passionate team members tend to be significantly more productive and creative

How do you stack up in your manager passions & core competencies? What are some of the other core competencies you feel a successful manager should possess? Start adding to the list below and score yourself as being either Ready to apply your core skills to being a manager, Developing your core skills or Insufficient to the task or skill identified. Remember that this list won't match anyone else's precisely and that is OK. Be as honest as you can. Lying to yourself only delays your acceptance of what others may already know.

CORE COMPETENCY	READY	DEVELOPING	INSUFFICIENT
Example: Rigorous Honesty	X		
Strong People Orientation			
Effective Communication Skills			
Patience & High Tolerance For Mistakes			
Rigorous Honesty			
Ability To Perform Simple Math Quickly			
Insight Into Human Behavior Patterns			
Commitment To Excellence			
High Stress Tolerance			
Unflinching Ethics			
Intermediate Skills With Office Software			

Leading Your Former Peers

If you are like most new managers, you have been promoted from within and you view your new responsibilities as a very public statement of confidence in you by senior leaders of your organization. Indeed, it is likely reasonable to assume that is the case. You undoubtedly have worked hard, perhaps for a number of years, in order to achieve that promotion to the leadership ranks of your organization. Earning that management job is an appropriate response to the commitment and dedication you've shown.

Achievements such as these are even sweeter when they can be shared with friends and co-workers. It is normal for you to want everyone you've worked side by side with over the years to be as happy for you as you and your family are. Unfortunately, that is not always what happens.

Many times new managers are completely astonished to discover that the friends they have made among their peers at work suddenly see them in a new (and often unflattering) light. Instead of back slaps they get cold shoulders. Instead of celebrating the accomplishment of getting promoted they are treated to quiet disdain or, worse yet, blatant disregard. This is not something that most new managers are not prepared for nor do they know how to respond.

The Four Stages of New Manager Grief

Because managers are human beings (despite what their subordinates might claim) they typically follow a predictable pattern of behavior when their former peers seemingly turn on them. The cycle goes something like this:

- Disbelief: You are simply astounded by the sort of animosity or cold indifference you are feeling from your friends at work. You cannot imagine that the same people you were joking with yesterday are suddenly tight-lipped and withdrawn when you come around. You rack your brain trying to figure out what you did to them that caused this change in your relationship.

- Anger: Now that it has started to sink in, you are beginning to get angry. Those who have apparently turned on you are the first to feel the heat of your response, often demonstrated by a reflexive veil of superiority and haughtiness on your part. Your attitude, although unspoken, bears a striking resemblance to a sort of childish "what is good for the goose is good for the gander" posture. You might even say things under your breath like "two can play at that game" or "they do not know who they are messing with." Your initial euphoria at being promoted has suddenly become bittersweet as you begin to contemplate how you will use your newfound authority to punish those who have turned their backs on you.

- Bitterness: Your anger and desire for retribution may get the better of you, clouding the judgment that helped to get you noticed by senior management in the first place. You may actually try to make an example of someone, only to discover that the HR Department won't allow you to exact revenge quite so frivolously   It is at this point that you realize that there are limits to the reach of your power and authority and that you probably only made matters worse by reacting so emotionally.

- Acceptance: This stage occurs when you have finally realized that, for better or worse, human nature is what has caused the rift between you and your former peers. With the passage of time you begin to understand that several factors, among them envy, insecurity and fear have been the instigators of the new type of relationship you have with your friends at work. Along with your acceptance comes a more stable and reasonable attitude toward of which your staff is aware and to which they respond. Everyone begins to settle in to the new reality of your leadership and refocuses on the work at hand.

The View From Up Here

One of the phenomena you experience when you assume your first management position is the sudden change in your perspective. How you viewed the work environment when you were a line employee is dramatically different from the scenery you now get as a manager. Things that used to annoy or anger you about "Management" have suddenly become much clearer. You now have an understanding of why a lot of things occurred—policy changes, personnel decisions, product direction—that you couldn't see from down in the trenches.

How does this happen? One of the most challenging things for you to do is to broaden your view of the workplace to encompass many things you never cared about (or even knew about) before. You must have a more "global" view of the organization that stretches beyond the boundaries of your own departmental domain. Despite the fact that your area of managerial control may be limited by function, division or some other organizational definition, as a good manager you must understand how your team fits into the overall picture. You must comprehend what the touch points are between your team and every other team – what happens when your team fails to deliver on its part of the equation? What happens to your team when someone else fails to deliver on their commitment? In short, a manager must understand intuitively the interdependencies that connect the organization to it.

To facilitate this new understanding, new managers must begin to grasp how things work in the universe beyond their reach. Getting a global view of the organization won't happen simply by sitting in their office minding their own store. Some practical steps to take include:

- Begin to develop a new peer group to replace the one you've left behind. Seek out your new management-level peers and spend time learning how their department functions. Go to lunch with them, have coffee in the morning with them or even set up a regularly scheduled meeting to discuss current issues and concerns.
- Talk to your own immediate supervisor about the "big picture" issues you have realized are so important to your success and the success of those around you. Senior managers have a vested interest in helping you to succeed, especially since they likely played a role in getting you promoted in the first place.
- Hold a joint "brown bag lunch" between your team and one or two other teams from different areas of the organization, encouraging attendees to share their perceptions of what the others contribute (and giving everyone a chance to clarify misconceptions).

The view from the management vantage point is different from just what can be seen on the front lines. It may help to think of this in the following way. As you begin to climb to higher heights within the organization, the horizon begins to change. If you think about how much more you can take in when you look out the window of a plane, first at ground level, then at 5000 feet up, then 10000, then 30000 and so on, you will have a true sense of how dramatically your view changes as you accept the ever greater responsibilities that come with being a manager.

Avoiding the Power Trip

It is a common misconception among new managers that they have, with their promotion, suddenly gotten to be "in control." Listen for enthusiastic statements such as "Now things will get better around here" and "I'm going to fix everything that is wrong in this department." Have you said things like this yourself? It is natural for new managers to believe that they exercise control over their people and processes. After all, that has been their perspective toward their own managers all along. Nothing could be further from reality

Control in an organization does NOT lie with management. Control of what goes on in an organization lies with the staff or line employees. Managers cannot truly control what their employees do. Remember our definition of management is "... *the process of influencing others to perform tasks and/or behave in a manner that they would not ordinarily do on their own.*" To manage effectively is to be a strong persuader of others. Consider that managers cannot actually prevent someone in their organization from making mistakes, deliberate or unintentional. The only person who controls what employees or subordinate does is employees. Therefore, if you are a new manager whose ego has swelled with ambitions of directly controlling everything in your department merely as a result of your new position, you are in for a rude awakening.

It can be somewhat humbling and, even, disappointing for a brand new manager to finally recognize that being the boss has very little to do with being "in charge" or "in control". Their expectations, biased by their own perceptions of managers they have known throughout their career, can be seriously compromised by this version of reality. If you are one of those new managers, do not despair. There is far more job satisfaction in successfully convincing someone to do something that benefits the organization than by attempting to force them into compliance.

This does not mean that you are powerless. What you do possess is the *authority* to back up your efforts at influencing desired behavior with specific outcomes or consequences, depending upon the situation. As a manager you may be given the authority, by virtue of your position, to determine how large or small employee's next pay raise will be. This is a tremendously powerful article of persuasion, one which must be used judiciously. So, despite the fact that you cannot directly control what your team members do, you have the means at your disposal, granted by the authority that your job classification of manager carries, to effectively persuade the staff to deliver the desired performance.

Giving Credit Where Credit Is Due
One of the greatest characteristics of successful managers is humility. It is an important factor in their daily interactions with their team and other teams beyond the boundaries of their responsibility, yet it is often ignored. Humility in this context refers to the desire of managers to deflect credit from them in order for it to be properly assigned to employees in their group. For example, when a front line employee in a manufacturing plant comes up with an idea that saves the company $.50 raw materials costs on every widget they produce, a manager should not accept the credit. Rather they should go out of their way to be certain that employees personally are recognized by senior management for the cost saving idea.

This may seem to be a trivial matter, but it is an essential tool in both employee morale and in helping managers avoid out of control egos. There are times when it is fully appropriate for managers to be recognized for positive contributions, such as when the managers themselves actually designed an improvement or achieved some new watershed benchmark. It is counterproductive, however, for managers to receive the credit for something that a frontline employee did. The potential for negative impacts to morale should be fairly obvious. What may not be easily apparent is the loss of confidence and trust of employees that the manager suffers as a result of being a "credit hog."

The rules are slightly different when applied to group efforts. Say that members of a sales department have not only met but exceeded their quota for the preceding accounting period. It is not something that was done by a single individual but rather is a result of the collective contributions of each member of the department. Should the Sales Manager accept the credit for the work of the field sales staff? The answer is...sort of. Remember that good managers are able to persuade the people under their supervision to achieve something that members of the department would not otherwise have done on their own. To that extent the sales manager deserves credit for skillfully managing the team to produce the desired results, but the actual accomplishment of closing increased numbers of sales should be credited to the specific sales person(s) involved. In this way, both manager and team members receive the appropriate credit for the work they have done.

Building Informal Networks among Your Staff
Much is being written these days about the power of networking, whether formally or informally. Formal networks are clusters of individuals with similar interests who participate in a highly structured "community," such as a Board of Directors or even online discussion groups. Informal networks, by contrast, have little of the structure and predictability offered by formal networks. Informal clustering of individuals can take the shape of a happy hour at the end of the workday or a pot luck picnic where there is little formal planning involved. In the workplace, there are both formal and informal networks (and each has its distinctive place). Formal networks inside an organization provide order and purpose to group activities. Informal networks can stimulate creativity and "big picture" thinking, either of which is a good thing for the group.

When your team members gather informally to "shoot the breeze" they are networking informally. In many cases individuals gather around one employee's desk or cubicle and talk about something directly related to work being performed by that person. The free flowing exchange of ideas can provide a fertile environment for innovative and unique solutions to evolve. As a manager you may see these types of gatherings as hurting productivity because of the distractions they cause. Be careful here. Do not act too hastily before you have a chance to understand the group dynamics at work. Are employees just kibitzing and wasting time or are they actually engaged in work related discussion? Shutting down the informal networks that spring up as a result of a collaborative work environment is counterproductive to efficiency and damaging to employee morale.

Encourage your employees to use informal networks to stimulate creativity and innovation. Be willing to tolerate what appears on the surface to be goofing off if what is really occurring will benefit the organization in the long run. Your manager's intuition should guide your determination of whether your team is abusing the privilege.

Management Accountability

Accountability Defined

> *Main Entry: ac·count·abil·i·ty*
> Pronunciation: \ə-ˌkau̇n-tə-ˈbi-lə-tē\
> Function: noun
> Date: 1794
> : the quality or state of being <u>accountable</u>; especially
> : an obligation or willingness to accept responsibility or to <u>account</u> for one's actions <public officials lacking accountability>
> "accountability." Merriam-Webster Online Dictionary. 2008. Merriam-Webster Online. 7October 2008<http://www.merriam-webster.com /dictionary/accountability>

Were you to survey several modern dictionaries you would find that the word "accountability" is generally described as the act of accepting responsibility for one's actions & decisions. This is a reasonable, if simple, definition, not only for individuals but also for those who serve in leadership roles in corporations and organizations. Personal accountability is frequently thought of in terms of how we behave ethically, morally and, in some circles, spiritually. It is mostly concerned with the decisions we make as distinct human beings and how those decisions impact others as well as ourselves.

Corporate accountability takes the concept of personal accountability one step further. Being accountable within an organization is identical to personal accountability when taken in its most granular form—that is to say when it is viewed purely within the context of one person's actions. However, when one individual is also accountable for the actions of others, the simplicity of the personal accountability context is replaced by the complexity of multiple instances of individual actions integrating with one another. *Put another way, corporate accountability imbues the manager with the burden of ownership for the collective actions of all those in their chain of authority.*

The implication of this on those in management positions is significant. Managers must be accountable for everything that occurs within their functional area or authority chain. Each successive management layer must, in turn, accept the burden of accountability for the actions of everyone under their area of responsibility. This means that those who sit at the very highest levels in an organization have accountability "exposure" for everything that occurs below them (within their defined chain of command).

When individuals become managers for the first time, it is not uncommon for them to be unaware of the hidden implications of their new assignment. Beyond the operational aspects of their new position, these new leaders have accepted, often without realizing it, total *ownership* of everything that happens in their department, *regardless of the cause or circumstances*. That last point is critical: too often new managers fail to understand that it is no longer acceptable for them to try to deflect blame onto others for the mistakes that are made within their functional area. Accountability for new managers is identical to that which governs senior, more experienced leaders. Managers are accountable for everything that goes on within their functional area, even those things which they may feel is out of their direct control. Before they assumed their leadership role, the new managers may very well have been able to avoid responsibility and/or blame for the actions, good or bad, of their peers. What these new supervisors must accept immediately is that defensive claims of "It is not my job!" have become a relic of their working past. As of their first day in their position, they are on the proverbial hot seat for a seemingly endless realm of possible problems. It is likely that brand new managers will be given some margin for error in the earliest days of their tenure, as they "come up to speed" with the new position they occupy. This won't last very long, however, before those accountable for the actions of new managers begin to demand more of them.

In practical terms, accountability means that new managers must accept whatever consequences result from the actions of those who report to them through the chain of command. In minor issues this may take the form of a rebuke or even a written warning by their immediate supervisor. In major issues being accountable can potentially result in managers actually losing their jobs. Accountability is not, therefore, a throwaway concept that new managers can blithely dismiss.

Accountability versus Responsibility

I believe that there is a very real difference between being responsible and being accountable. Responsibility is all about the execution of specific tasks—tasks which are (or should be) defined in a job description. In other words, being responsible for a task simply means that you or the person in the specific role you occupy is required to perform that task. Accepting the distinction may require you to rewire your thinking, if you are open to a new mindset.

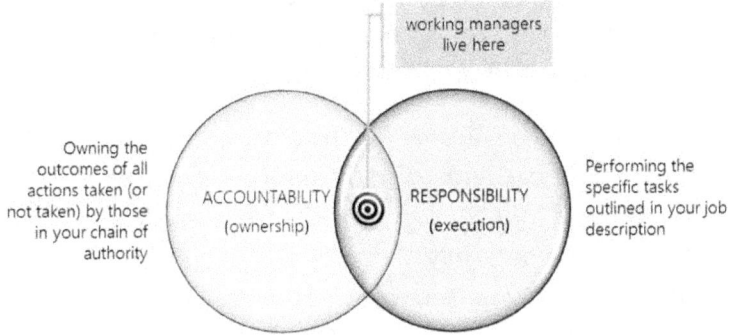

As the diagram suggests, "working" managers – those who are expected to perform specific tasks – are both accountable and responsible for what they do. In truth, so is every employee regardless of where they fall in the organizational hierarchy. Frontline staff who have no direct reports fall into this category, with the added benefit that they don't have to be accountable for anyone else's actions.

The Accountability versus Control Trap

Let's step back for a moment to consider an apparent contradiction. In the previous section titled "Avoiding the Power Trip," we reviewed the notion that managers realistically have no control over the actions of their employees. Employees will do what they will do because, in most cases, there is no means for physically preventing them from acting in a given manner. Managers are charged with exerting sufficient and effective influence over employees to motivate them to do whatever is the next right thing.

Given this situation, new managers may feel they are truly in a trap. They cannot really control the actions of their employees, yet they are expected to be fully accountable for whatever those actions are. Human nature being what it is, at some point in their management career these leaders will be caught in this trap. Someone within their organization will act in a way that is directly counter to the best interests of the company and the training they've received. Some managers may be caught completely off guard by the circumstances of this deviation from the norm, yet being unaware of such circumstances does not provide an excuse for them to avoid suffering the consequences.

> *In 2008, the USS George Washington, one of the Nimitz-class aircraft carriers of the US navy, was forced to put into dry dock for $70 million worth of repairs made necessary because of a fire on board while at sea. While several sailors were injured in the accident, none perished. The ship was under repair for several months at a time when the USA was fighting two wars overseas. Since aircraft carriers are one of the most powerful weapons in our arsenal and a visible extension of American foreign*

*policy and military capabilities, the removal from
active duty of the Washington and her crew was no
small matter. When all of the dust had settled and
the investigation into the fire completed, only two
crew members were relieved of duty. Who do you
think it was?*

If you picked anyone other than the captain and executive officer – the
equivalent of the CEO and COO – go back and reread this section. They
were relieved of their command and likely reassigned to a desk job for
the duration of their careers. Is this fair? Absolutely! When you ascend
to a leadership role in any organization, large or small, you acknowledge
that you understand that management isn't a reward or perk for being a
great person. Management is a burden, one which you must be willing
to bear. If you don't want to own the outcome of everything your team
does (or doesn't do), then spare yourself some heartache and the
company some turmoil and move on from leadership.

Succeeding Through Accepting Accountability
Given what we have just discussed concerning accountability, it is vital to
point out that being accountable is not a lose/lose proposition. To the
contrary, a healthy respect for their own accountability can be the best
friend of new managers. Why? There are two fundamental reasons: 1)
managers who know and accept the scope and nature of their
accountability will actively <u>influence</u> their employees to always do what
is right and to learn well from their occasional (and unavoidable)
mistakes: 2) managers who demonstrate that they are not afraid of the
inherent challenges of true accountability will be considered an
enormously valuable corporate asset and will, over time, be held in ever
increasing regard by senior management.

Beyond these, there is a more tangible reason for accepting
accountability in earnest, especially for managers who work for publicly
traded companies. The high profile nature of significant cases of
corporate malfeasance (e.g. Enron, Adelphia Cable, Halliburton) has

heightened market and regulatory sensitivity to such mismanagement. In most of these cases, the offending behavior can be traced to a failure of the culture of accountability within the organization. Such an environment is like a Petri dish for breeding managerial complacency.

Accountability is at once both a simple concept and a challenging mission. To be accountable simply means that you accept the consequences for the actions of those under your supervision without offering excuses. Just as military leaders can lose their command assignment because of the actions of the lowest ranking members of their command, so too a new manager must realize that the true nature of the position to which they've risen is one fraught with risk that can only be reduced by employing sound, practical management practices.

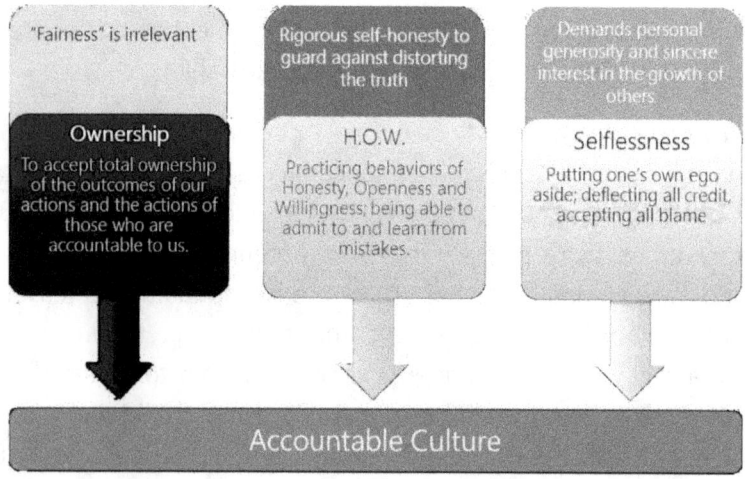

"Fairness" is irrelevant	Rigorous self-honesty to guard against distorting the truth	Demands personal generosity and sincere interest in the growth of others
Ownership	H.O.W.	Selflessness
To accept total ownership of the outcomes of our actions and the actions of those who are accountable to us.	Practicing behaviors of Honesty, Openness and Willingness; being able to admit to and learn from mistakes.	Putting one's own ego aside; deflecting all credit, accepting all blame

Accountable Culture

Getting Started
Accountability as a culture will not develop on its own. As with most other characteristics of the organization, the example of accountability flows from the top down. If the necessary buy-in (walking the talk) exists at the executive level of the company it becomes easier to convince employees that they, too, should embrace the concept of being accountable. If there is no acceptance of the practices of accountability

at the C-level, it is likely that attaining enterprise wide cooperation will fail. It may still be possible within a single department, but the moment it becomes necessary for accountable behaviors to cross functional lines all bets are off.

Starting the process of instilling a culture of accountability begins with assessing whether the company has the fundamental building blocks in place (albeit not necessarily formalized).

- Does the company have clearly defined roles for each position? Are there job descriptions, documented processes, clear lines of authority and reporting, etc.?
- Are managers required to spell out, in explicit terms, what their expectations are for their team members? An employee should be able to recite what is expected of them at any time—anything less negatively impacts their chance of accountability success. This includes training of existing employees as well as new hire indoctrination procedures.
- Are there any accountability systems in place or available that can be used to monitor and measure how successfully the company is living up to the accountability mantra? There are likely quite a number of these systems in place already, perhaps not viewed as part of larger whole. Collect these metrics into an accountability scorecard and regularly communicate the results.
- What consequences (positive and negative) are spelled out in response to outcomes? This is where it becomes challenging for many organizations. Outcomes without consequences, regardless of positive or negative, are only mildly valuable. It must be clearly understood by all involved that there are going to be consequences based on outcomes that each employee must "own".

Before attempting to lead the organization to an accountability posture be certain that the building blocks are not only developed but also viewed as creditable—in other words, do the employees and managers and executives take them seriously? You might observe that this seems like a classic "chicken and egg" problem; how can something be viewed as creditable if it hasn't yet been implemented?   The answer to the contradiction is quite simple and direct.   If the company adopts and adheres to policies and procedures that support the concepts of accountability prior to a formalized push for an accountability culture, management performance will lend the required creditability to these building blocks.   Only then can accountability be realized not as a policy or program, but rather as a corporate instinct.

Defined Roles – WHO is performing which tasks, functions, processes, etc. -- *Job descriptions, process definitions, information flow*

Explicit Expectations – WHAT is expected from each member of the team -- *Project plans, directives, correspondence*

Accountability Systems – TOOLS & METRICS *used to monitor and report on performance, behaviors, etc. -- Performance Reviews, Production Reports, Financials, Customer Satisfaction surveys*

Defined Consequences – OUTCOMES & ACTIONS *which are communicated to all stakeholders -- Bonuses, Write-ups, promotions, terminations*

Delegation

DELEGATE - verb

1. To entrust to another <delegate authority>
2. To appoint as one's representative [4]

One of the more enjoyable aspects of becoming a manager is that you are no longer required or expected to personally perform all of the necessary work to accomplish a given task. Indeed, as has been previously discussed, management is about successfully influencing others to perform tasks they would not ordinarily do on their own. The intersection of the first point with the second is what constitutes management delegation: influencing others to do what you would ordinarily do, but cannot do now because of your expanded responsibilities. Having the ability to delegate is one of the objects of a manager's authority.

Delegation is, in fact, the product of all of our management practices. If we consistently operate from a mindset along these lines we can expect delegation to be among the least of our concerns from day to day. In the end, it all comes down to trust.

It sounds so easy and straightforward to say that managers can simply delegate jobs or units of work to those who report to them. The principle is simple enough to grasp. Experience has shown, however, that delegation is one of the toughest challenges new managers face. Frequently, new managers are unconvinced that their staff is capable of getting the work done to the level of quality that is expected or that the situation demands. This is usually the result of a lack of confidence and trust on the part of managers in employees who would be performing the work. This "confidence gap" can occur regardless of whether new managers are assuming the role from an external position or accepting a promotion from within the organization. Knowing the staff personally is not a mitigating factor in establishing an atmosphere of trust.

The Confidence Gap

New managers want to succeed. They want to be seen succeeding, as well. This personal drive for positive recognition is one of the factors which feed the confidence gap. Anytime managers sense that their employees are either incapable or unmotivated to help bring the work in on time, on budget and on target, they will take unto themselves full responsibility for actually producing the work in question. This is sometimes doable, despite the demands of the manager role, especially when it occurs in the early days of their tenure. There will be periods of reduced work when managers actually have the cycles to jump in with both hands and feet. This time luxury quickly fades, however, the longer managers are in the position, ironically because they have actually been successful in completing the tasks. The resulting glowing reports have the unintended effect of heaping many more projects on their plate, thereby making it impossible for the manager to be successful for a second time. At some point in this Catch-22 timeline, managers are either forced to delegate some or all of the workload to their employees or, less desirable, they must admit to not being able to get everything done effectively and efficiently. In some cases, managers will substantially fail to deliver on promised milestones, leaving their peers and superiors to wonder about the wisdom of having put them into the job to begin with.

The No-Dumping Rule

Beyond the confidence gap, new managers can fail to delegate out of a sincere reluctance to "dump on" those former peers who now report to them. They will rationalize that their buddy Tom, with whom they just went bowling last Monday night, is already swamped with work and to give him more would be a disaster. So they look around the employee bullpen for the next best choice to delegate the work to and, finding none that are as good as Tom, they decide that they are the only one qualified to do the job. Once again, up come the sleeves and down goes their productivity as managers. The no-dumping mindset, borne out of a genuine desire to protect their personal relationships with their former coworkers, becomes a trap that ensnares managers.

Once again, the irony in this situation is that by trying to protect their employees from too much work (and, therefore, too much stress), new managers are actually creating a more stressful environment to work in. This occurs for two reasons:

- Managers suddenly experience an outsized level of stress owing to the unexpected demand for their time in carrying out the work they cannot (or won't) delegate. Unintentionally, they can project their high stress levels onto the rest of the staff, sowing discord and resentment and, ultimately, impacting critical operational areas of the organization.
- Employees can begin to misinterpret the benevolent nature of managerial unwillingness to give them additional tasks and, instead, interpret the message to be that they are not trusted (which is a distinct possibility). This becomes a confidence gap in reverse where employees begin to lose confidence in the leadership potential of their managers.

Practical Organizational Impacts

While less obvious to the casual observer, there are nevertheless broader implications to the failure of a manager to adequately delegate. Below is a short list of negative outcomes that can impact the organization's success:

- When employees are never entrusted with new and challenging initiatives they become jaded and unhappy. The resulting turnover is costly and disruptive to productivity and morale.
- Employees who have been allowed to tackle delegated tasks will build on their own experiences and develop confidence and bench strength for the organization.
- Managers are limiting their own chances for advancement within the organization when they fail to delegate tasks to subordinates. When managers themselves are under consideration for a higher level position within the organization, they may be ignored or passed over because of their failure to build an effective team behind them.

- One of the ways in which managers are evaluated for effectiveness is by monitoring how easy or difficult it would be to replace that person, should they leave. Essentially, managers are at their philosophical best when they are preparing their employees to succeed them. Never investing the time necessary to adequately train employees to take over managerial responsibilities is a fundamental mistake. It may provide short term job security for managers, but in the longer term the managers may be perceived as too insecure to assume ever increasing levels of trust from their superiors.

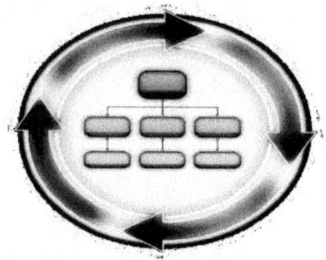

Tips for Effective Delegating
Ronald Reagan is quoted as saying "Surround yourself with the best people you can find, delegate authority and do not interfere." While Reagan was sometimes chided for not having a strong command of the details of the policies and programs advanced by his administration, his managerial philosophy was on target nonetheless. It is almost impossible in a technology-driven, interconnected world for any one person to stay on top of everything needed to know about an industry. Managers are most effective when they understand and accept that delegation is a key strategy in organizational success.

There are countless management books available that discuss the art of delegation to precise levels of detail. For the new manager, it is better to come to grips with some basic tips for becoming better at delegation:

- Review job descriptions to know what each employee's expectations are. Any employee who does not fully understand the scope of their responsibilities (and accountabilities) is likely to fail when a mission critical task is delegated to them. Be sure that both you and the employee are in agreement as to what is expected of them.

- Align the authority of those you delegate to with the necessities of the job. Giving someone a task without the appropriate amount of authority is setting them up to fail—or at the very least setting you up to fail as a manager.
- Act as facilitator to insure that employees have all the tools they need. It is important to verify that the employee isn't trying to achieve the established objectives with one arm tied behind their back. Get them whatever they need or help them identify alternative strategies if what they need is not going to be available.
- Once delegated, let the employee do the job without oppressive supervision. If you've made the right choice of individuals to delegate to, they should not need to be micro-managed. If you are unable to let go of the reigns the employee will quickly become demotivated to take on larger tasks with bigger accountabilities.

Delegation demands of new managers several leaps of faith. First, they must put away their distrust of delegation fed by their own self-centered motives for success. Second, they must believe that employees to whom they are delegating important work are capable of succeeding. Setting up employees to fail because of ill-considered delegation borders on irresponsible management. Effective delegation grows the staff, the manager and the company as a whole.

In the end, it all just boils down to trust. The manager must be confident that they can trust the employee to "get it done" correctly and on time. If there is any doubt in the managers' mind that will likely be transmitted to the employee. The employee needs to be able trust that the manager will give them room to navigate, including a reasonable tolerance for making the wrong choices. Those who are unable to exhibit genuine trust in their fellows ought to consider this basic premise—either the manager is not qualified or the staff is not qualified. In either case, the resulting distrust can be lethal to the morale of the manager and the employees.

Decision Making Methods

"A decision is the action an executive must take when he has information so incomplete that the answer does not suggest itself." -- Admiral Arthur W Radford, USN   Time 25 Feb 57

As Admiral Radford said, decisions must be made whenever the proper course to take in a given situation is not obvious. Management is, in many ways, fueled primarily by the need for someone to make decisions in times of uncertainty. If every path were clear it would be a simple matter for workers to follow it, with a reasonable expectation of success each time, provided that adequate training has been provided to employees.

Of course, we know that every path is not clear to us. Every single day of our lives we must make decisions, both personally and professionally, about enormously diverse matters that face us. When we are young adults we make decisions about what to wear, where to go to college, who to date, etc. Many of these personal decisions have only minor impact on our lives or the lives of others. When we enter the working world, however, we find we have a thousand new decisions to make that frequently can have major implications for ourselves and those with whom we work.

It is this latter condition which managers must contend with. Many times managers are doing nothing but making decisions throughout the course of their day. In fact, often young or newly promoted executives are struck by the notion that all they seem to do is make decisions. Management is fundamentally about making choices on behalf of the organization. It generally does not produce a specific unit of work (at least not in the "classical" sense).

It is not oversimplifying to state that, in order for new managers to be successful, they must be able to make decisions. It is not as straightforward a process as it may appear, especially for brand new managers.

Method to the Madness
Effective decision making is not accomplished through the flip of a coin. If it were, anyone could be a manager because every choice would have only two options—heads or tails—with little to no consideration given to the environmental aspects of the situation requiring the decision. For us as managers, decision making demands a more comprehensive perspective than the stark simplicity of two sides of a coin. (Although there will always be times when a choice is very clearly between just two options, it does not mean that making the right choice is settled merely by letting "fate" be the guide.) Managers are required to think much more broadly than that. They must be driven by the desire to make the best decision they possibly can, given all of the variables that can impact the choice.

How then do we make good decisions? The answer lies in the consistent application of a standard process every time a decision is required. Managers who learn to rely on the process, rather than guessing or hoping for the best, are destined to make the right choices far more often than not during their career. The four steps in this process are 1) Develop options to choose from; 2) Infuse creativity to uncover new approaches; 3) Evaluate the short and long term implications of the decision; and 4) Make the call.

Develop Options
The most important activity of the decision making process is the development of options. Having options to choose from is sometimes more difficult than it might seem to be, on the surface. Identifying multiple pathways to take for a given situation requires

- strong observation skills--the ability to grasp what is right in front of you
- determination—a highly focused will to get it right
- stubbornness--the ability to not accept the easiest or most obvious choice
- curiosity--the ability to go beyond the obvious to uncover the root causes of events/circumstances

Developing options demands that managers not be satisfied with only limited choices. A good decision results from having the most information available to base the choice on. Sometimes this requires additional research, beyond what is readily observable, hence the demand for intellectual curiosity. Managers with a strong will to "get it right" will seldom reach for the easiest alternative, even when it seems as though further research is unwarranted. Often, more research is essential in order to eliminate alternatives from consideration as much as it is to introduce additional alternatives. In such cases, managers will need to be able to anticipate potential outcomes of taking a given path, carefully identifying the multitude of variables that tend to sway the result in one direction or another.

Getting to the variables which influence the outcome of a particular course requires that managers decompose the situation into all its constituent parts. This means taking the problem or circumstance apart (intellectually, not physically--unless there is a mechanical component that would justify such action) to examine each piece by itself and within the context of its role in the larger picture. This is an important aspect of the options development cycle because it forces managers to examine many possible courses of action and/or outcomes. It does not guarantee that they will uncover every alternative, though many will based on their instinctive knowledge of their field; however, it does force them to open their thinking to new possibilities.

Infuse Creativity

When managers thoroughly decompose a required decision into its "atomic" parts, the door is opened to the next step in the decision making process--infusing creativity. With all of the trace elements of a problem laid out before them, managers have a tremendous opportunity to try to rearrange the puzzle pieces to see if they can craft a unique answer or decision. By applying creativity to the situation, managers may potentially uncover decision options that might otherwise never have come to light. The key to infusing creativity is tearing down the emotional and intellectual walls we build between ourselves and the sea of decision alternatives that exist. This is certainly much easier to say than it is to do, yet it is fundamental to the success of managers trying to make the right decisions. Infusing creativity does not require great artistic talent to be effective. It does, however, require an unflinching willingness to consider options that may seem unrealistic or even silly at first glance. By utilizing a process of elimination we can distinguish those alternatives which actually make sense from those that are unworkable or too fanciful. Those that remain after creativity is infused are then combined with those which were readily apparent to construct a comprehensive, option-rich set of choices for managers to work from.

Evaluate the Short and Long-Term Implications
Every decision has repercussions, sometimes good, other times not so good. Likewise, every decision has both a short - and long-term impact on the organization, marketplace, competition, etc. The short-term impacts should be readily apparent. I not, it is an indication that adequate due diligence consideration of the options available was not performed. When this occurs the remedy is straightforward. Go back to the options development stage and start again.

In many cases the long term impacts won't be visible or even easy to imagine, yet they are there nonetheless. The mission of managers is to apply the context of time to all of the options developed in the previous step so that they may better anticipate how the various stakeholders will respond to the decision that is made. Despite being more difficult to predict, analyzing the long term eventualities which result from the decisions we make is critical to making better choices.

Equally important is for a manager to know what the broader impacts of a given decision may be. Managers must evaluate the implications of their decisions not only on their own area of accountability but also on other disparate, yet interconnected constituencies. This may not result in the elimination of a particular option that could have a negative effect on others, but it will serve to enlighten those stakeholders involved as to the potential downstream impacts that might result from the decision(s) made.

Make the Call

By this point in the decision making process managers have identified options; they have infused creativity into those options to discover even more alternatives and they have assessed the impacts of those options within the context of time and reach. They have only one thing left to do. Decide! While this may sound like an incredibly obvious thing to say, this is an area were many well-intentioned managers fail to execute. Despite having gathered all of the information possible to aid in their decision, despite having gone to great lengths to creatively "think outside the box" and despite casting a far-reaching eye on the future, managers are always faced with the one defining moment when they actually have to pick which course to take. What they must now rely on is their own instinct and self-confidence in order to advance and finish the decision making process.

In some organizations, new managers may be reluctant to make a clear decision out of fear of being wrong and subsequently suffering significant career damage as a result. In others, there may be a sense that taking the risk of actually deciding something that might not work out exactly as anticipated is too great a trial of their need to always be "right" in their supervisor's eyes. In still others, it may be that new managers are told to make decisions and, when they try to do so, they are consistently overridden by a control-centric supervisor who never learned how to effectively delegate[5]. Regardless of these possible circumstances, decisions still need to be made by those who are given the authority to manage people, processes and resources. Doing nothing is an option (sometimes even a viable one), but it does not help the image and reputation of new managers who rely on this alternative too often. New managers must be confident in their adherence to a stable decision making process and their egos must be adaptive to the inevitable mistakes or errors in judgment that all new managers make.

So the only directive is to "make the call". Using all of the tools at their disposal the new manager must make a decision--good or bad, for better or worse—in order to advance the objectives of the organization. New managers who are paralyzed with indecision will not succeed, guaranteed. Their supervisors will quickly recognize that their promotion to manager was a mistake and, as supervisor, they now have an obligation to find another candidate for the position (or even do it themselves). In any case, not being able to make decisions is management career suicide. If you are capable of making decisions readily then you have nothing to fear by using the process outlined in this chapter.

If, however, you are struggling with making a choice regardless of how much empirical evidence or experience in the field you've amassed, please pay heed to this suggestion: just do it!

Decision making is about options, alternatives and evidence. But it also has a different dynamic at work—one which cannot be quantified or bestowed on a manager. That dynamic is the ability of managers to acknowledge that they have done all that they could possibly do in order to make the right decision, thereby enabling them to step out in faith and make the call.

Food For Thought

If you are paralyzed and unable to make decisions because of a fear of failure, remember that the only real failures are the ones from which we refuse to learn. Throughout your management career you will make lots of mistakes and bad decisions. Do not dwell on them. Instead, consider them as valuable teachers and forge ahead. If you are struggling through the consequences of a previously unwise decision the best approach is to charge ahead and make a better

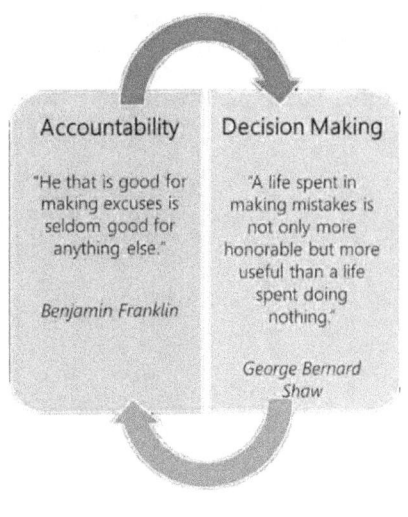

Accountability

"He that is good for making excuses is seldom good for anything else."

Benjamin Franklin

Decision Making

"A life spent in making mistakes is not only more honorable but more useful than a life spent doing nothing."

George Bernard Shaw

choice. In other words, accelerate into the turns that will inevitably come during your time as a manager. You will get to the other side of the problem much faster and find it easier to accept that no one is 100% right in everything they do.

Understanding Financial Statements

"There are plenty of ways to get ahead. The first is so basic I'm almost embarrassed to say it: spend less than you earn." - Paul Clitheroe, Financial Commentator

One of the aspects of organizational management that many new managers are minimally conversant in is business finance and accounting, or, collectively, what we call "management economics." Unless you have a particular aptitude for the "money counting" side of the organization you may find the whole issue to be confusing at best and overwhelming at worst. You aren't alone. Quite a few new managers have never had any exposure to the numbers side of their organization, either because it wasn't a necessary part of their previous positions or because upper management chose to keep such information private. Yet these challenging subjects are the ones that, ultimately, matter the most to an organization, largely because driving a team toward an objective that results in measurable benefits (higher sales or profits, lower costs, etc.) is the essence of effective management. Indeed, without the ability to measure and report the progress of the group's efforts toward their common goals, managers would find their capacity to influence employees to certain behaviors and performance levels to be significantly reduced.

Let's accept as fact, then, that managers must have a fundamental understanding of management economics. For this training course to thoroughly educate new managers in the intricacies of finance and accounting that apply to their particular job would be nearly impossible, especially given the infinite variability of such matters from company (or organization) to company. Extensive studies would be required to gain an in-depth knowledge of these subjects—something that entire college degree programs are devoted to. In this course, we will instead focus on several universal concepts and skills which are likely to be required of new managers at some point.

Getting the Meanings Right

What I refer to as management economics is not actually related to the general science of economics as you may have heard it discussed in the media (terms like "economic policy, Federal Reserve and gross domestic product come to mind). For my purpose, I've chosen to use the phrase "management economics" as a collective means of referring to the areas of finance (cash management, contracts, shareholder relationships, etc.) and accounting (collecting and reporting on organizational performance). In most small to mid-sized businesses and other entities of similar size these functions are usually carried out by the same group of employees typically referred to as the Accounting Department. Because these topics are really about distinctly different tasks, regardless of their being lumped together under one department name, we feel it is helpful to create an encompassing category for them, hence the term management economics. Think of it as the money side of being a manager, whether in a private, public or non-profit organization.

Here are some key definitions you should get comfortable with:

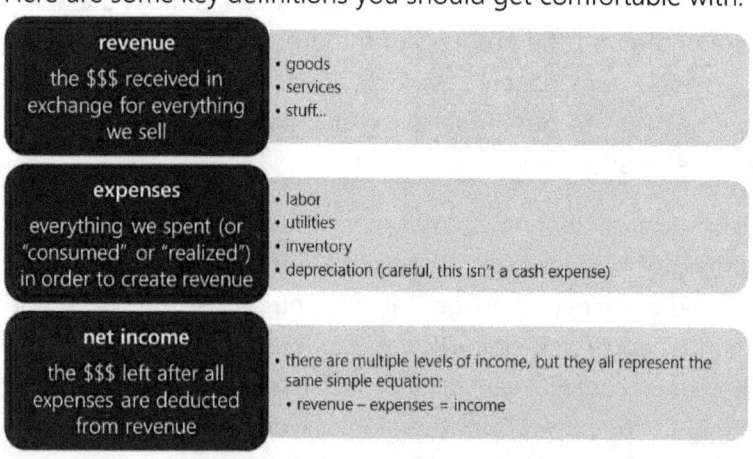

revenue
the $$$ received in exchange for everything we sell
- goods
- services
- stuff...

expenses
everything we spent (or "consumed" or "realized") in order to create revenue
- labor
- utilities
- inventory
- depreciation (careful, this isn't a cash expense)

net income
the $$$ left after all expenses are deducted from revenue
- there are multiple levels of income, but they all represent the same simple equation:
- revenue – expenses = income

assets all of the things we own or directly control that have real value	• property • equipment • CASH! • promises to pay made by customers or other interested parties
liabilities everything we owe to people and other organizations	• bills we need to pay • loans we are liable for • promises to pay we've made to vendors or other interested parties
owners' equity the dollar value of everything the organization owes to the owner(s)	• funds provided by the owners to start or maintain the organization's operations • can be private company owners or public company shareholders • retained earnings (net income that has not been used or paid-out to owners/employees, etc.)

Starting With the End: Financial Reporting

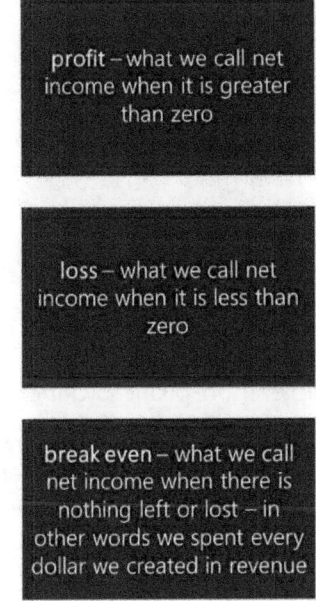

profit – what we call net income when it is greater than zero

loss – what we call net income when it is less than zero

break even – what we call net income when there is nothing left or lost – in other words we spent every dollar we created in revenue

We'll begin with a simple concept: profit. Profit is the amount of money left over—either in real cash or as a conceptual value represented on a financial report (more about that later), after all expense outflows (costs, grants, program funding, etc.) are deducted from all revenue inflows (sales, tax receipts, donations, etc). The most common means of communicating the news about organizational profits (or losses) is via a financial report called the Income Statement (also known as the Profit & Loss or P&L Statement). Sometimes non-financial managers will be heard to ask something like "How much money did we make?" To the listener who is familiar with corporate finance and accounting, this is the same as asking "how much profit did we generate?" In many such cases what the individual was really asking was what level of revenue (or sales) was reached. That may seem like an oversimplification or even a silly example to those who have some understanding of management economics but it is a misconception held more commonly than might be expected, especially among those new managers who have been promoted up through the ranks, perhaps without having taken any college-level business courses in accounting or finance.

There are most assuredly differences in the types of financial objectives that are important to each of the sectors mentioned (public, private and non-profit). For example, non-profit organizations are not usually concerned with generating more revenue than costs, especially since the special tax benefits afforded to such groups are predicated on the premise that what is taken in is to be used toward the benevolent mission of the group. The very prinicple is to reach equilibrium between them. Regardless of the type of organization, whenever revenues equal expenses this balance is referred to as "break-even," meaning no profits or losses resulted from business activity. Public entities are also less likely to deliberately pursue a profit; however these groups are occasionally able to show a "surplus" (just another word for profit) when they haven't spent everything on public services that they have taken in. Finally,

Revenue		
	Sales $	100,000
Expenses		
	Raw Materials $	50,000
	Salaries $	25,000
	Rent $	12,000
	Utilities $	6,000
	Total Expenses $	93,000
	Profit (Loss) $	7,000

private companies are almost exclusively focused on generating real profits as a result of their business activity. These organizations want to generate more revenue from selling their goods and services than they spend in order to create and market those goods and services.

Profit and cash are also sometimes thought of as being the same thing. They are distinctly different items. The amount of cash which an organization accumulates is referred to as its cash flow. In some cases an organization can show a particular level of profit on the income statement without actually having that much cash left over. This happens when revenue generated is spent on acquiring assets (equipment, property, etc.) that have a long expected life. Because they are expected to have a useful life beyond the current calendar period being represented on the income statement, such assets are not counted as immediately recognized direct expenses like salaries and rent. Rather they are classified as investments and hence, they do not show up on the income statement as a cost to the business. Instead they are seen on what is called a balance sheet: a financial report so named because it depicts the balance between assets and liabilities (financial obligations) held by the organization. As the name implies, assets and liabilities need to be in balance. That is to say that the collective value of all assets held, including cash in the bank, sales that have been made but have not yet been paid for by customers and long term physical hard goods acquired must equal the value of all liabilities recognized. The liabilities include outstanding bills the organization owes and shareholder or owner equity, which is the dollar amount representing the portion of a company's assets that the shareholders own outright versus that which has been borrowed. Equity is, in effect, an obligation that the company has to the shareholders or owners. Equity is actually calculated by subtracting liabilities from assets, thereby creating the "balance" intended.

For-profit groups have another measure that is reported on the balance sheet as part of the total liabilities portion. That category is called "retained earnings." As the name suggests, this category tracks the amount of earnings that accrue over time. Retained earnings can be either positive (when there are real profits) or negative (when there are losses). They are reported on the liabilities side of the balance sheet because they are an obligation that the company has to the owners in the form of profits that have accumulated from financial period to financial period. In theory, the company owes these accumulated profits to the owners, who could choose to take them out of the business as cash payouts rather than reinvesting them in the business to support growth.

Non-profit groups must be in balance because in order to be a non-profit they are obligated to disburse as much money as they take in – either through direct expenses such as salaries and rent and utilities or as grants, subsidies, etc. that are the whole point of the existence of the non-profit entity. Public organizations are similarly charged with providing

Assets			
	Cash on Hand	$	50,000
	Accounts Receivable	$	75,000
	Plant, Building & Equipment	$	500,000
	Total Current Assets	**$**	**625,000**
Liabilities			
	Accounts Payable	$	40,000
	Bank Loans Balance	$	20,000
	Total Current Liabilities	**$**	**60,000**
Equity			
	Retained Earnings	$	250,000
	Shareholder Equity	$	315,000
	Total Liabilities & Equity	**$**	**625,000**

services in exchange for the tax revenues they receive. When they do not spend as much as they take in they are said to have a surplus. This surplus revenue is represented on the balance sheet as well. It may simply be labeled as "Surplus" instead of Retained Earnings or it may be buried inside a host of other complex entries that public agencies are required to report. Surpluses are favorite tools of politicians for demonstrating their concern for their constituents because they can be used to justify cutting taxes.

The Supremacy of Cash

So what about cash? For most small to midsized organizations there is but one absolute when planning for growth. Cash is king! Think about it for a moment. Regardless of what the income statement tells us about profits or what assets the balance sheet may report on, the number one fuel that drives these organizations forward is cash. Access to cash is what allows managers to hire more staff, purchase new computers, pay the monthly rent and on and on. Even those entities which have access to cash through debt instruments like credit lines or direct loans still need cash to satisfy the regular payments that need to be made to keep these liabilities viable. Every organization must understand where its cash is coming from, both historically and looking ahead. The financial report which gives this vital data is called the Statement of Cash Flows or simply "cash flow statement." The cash flow statement shows precisely where cash is coming from, where it is being consumed and how successful the business is in generating cash to support operations in general.

Cash from Operations			
	Received from customers	$ 50,000	
	Paid to vendors	$ (15,000)	
	Paid to employees	$ (18,000)	
	Paid to support operations	$ (6,000)	
	Paid for interest & taxes	$ (2,500)	
	Net cash provided (consumed) by operating activities		$ 8,500
Cash from Investments			
	Received from sale of plant & equipment	$ 13,000	
	Received from sale of business units	$ -	
	Received from loans to officers	$ 500	
	Paid for new plant & equipment	$ (5,000)	
	Paid to buy business units	$ -	
	Net cash provided (consumed) by investing activities		$ 8,500
Cash from Financing			
	Received from issuing stock	$ -	
	Received from long-term debt	$ -	
	Paid to retire long-term debt	$ (3,500)	
	Paid for dividends	$ -	
	Net cash provided (consumed) by financing activities		$ (3,500)
	Increase (Decrease) in cash during period		$ 13,500
	Cash at beginning of period		$ 1,275
	Cash at end of period		$14,775

Being able to forecast cash flow is equally important for the manager. Planning for future purchases, new hiring, business acquisitions, etc., can only be reliably completed when there is a clear picture of where the cash will come from to pay for it all. Admittedly, cash flow projections rely on estimates of sales and expenses rather than the precision of the historical view, but these estimates should be based on experience over the years of operation (combined with expectations for the future) so there is an element of accuracy inherent in them. Coming up with projections is something we'll address in a later chapter.

Cash From Operations	Q1	Q2	Q3	Q4	Total
Received from customers	$ 50,000	$ 65,000	$ 66,300	$ 82,875	$264,175
Paid to vendors	$(15,000)	$(17,500)	$(17,850)	$(22,313)	$(72,663)
Paid to employees	$(18,000)	$(16,900)	$(17,238)	$(21,548)	$(73,686)
Paid to support operations	$ (6,000)	$ (8,900)	$ (9,078)	$(11,348)	$(35,326)
Paid for interest & taxes	$ (2,500)	$ (300)	$ (306)	$ (383)	$ (3,489)
Net cash provided (consumed) by operating activities	$ 8,500	$ 21,400	$ 21,828	$ 27,283	$ 79,011
Cash From Investments					
Received from sale of plant & equipment	$ 13,000	$ 1,200	$ -	$ 1,000	$ 15,200
Received from sale of business units	$ -	$ -	$ -	$ -	$ -
Received from loans to officers	$ 500	$ 500	$ 500	$ 500	$ 2,000
Paid for new plant & equipment	$ (5,000)	$ (350)	$ (4,100)	$ -	$ (9,450)
Paid to buy business units	$ -	$ -	$ -	$ -	$ -
Net cash provided (consumed) by investing activities	$ 8,500	$ 1,350	$ (3,600)	$ 1,500	$ 7,750
Cash From Financing					
Received from issuing stock	$ -	$ -	$ -	$ -	$ -
Received from long-term debt	$ -	$ -	$ -	$ -	$ -
Paid to retire long-term debt	$ (3,500)	$ (3,500)	$ (3,500)	$ (3,500)	$(14,000)
Paid for dividends	$ -	$ -	$ -	$ -	$ -
Net cash provided (consumed) by financing activities	$ (3,500)	$ (3,500)	$ (3,500)	$ (3,500)	$(14,000)
Increase (Decrease) in cash during period	$ 13,500	$ 19,250	$ 14,728	$ 25,283	$ 72,761
Cash at beginning of period	$ 1,275	$ 14,775	$ 34,025	$ 48,753	$ 1,275
Cash at end of period	$ 14,775	$ 34,025	$ 48,753	$ 74,036	$ 74,036

[53]

Financial Data At Work

"Do not seek for information of which you cannot make use." - Anna C. Brackett, Author

Putting Financial Information to Work

In the previous lesson we discussed the primary financial reports that provide insight into the overall performance of an organization. To review, they are the Income Statement (revenues versus expenses), the Balance Sheet (assets versus liabilities) and the Statement of Cash Flows (ability to generate cash to sustain the organization). While the information in these reports is vital to understand as managers, it is sometimes difficult to draw any conclusions or develop an informed opinion about what the metrics really mean in the larger scheme of things.

What makes this task easier is having the ability to understand and develop a series of key financial measures known as financial ratios. These ratios are relatively simple to construct yet provide invaluable glimpses into the true financial health of an organization and how well it is being managed.

Financial Ratio Categories

In general, there are four primary categories of financial ratios which are used in analyzing organization performance. Each of the various metrics inside each category is focused on a different management problem. The four categories are

- Financial Health (also known as Liquidity)
- Profitability
- Financial Leverage
- Productivity

There are actually a great many types of ratios which can be created to measure organization performance, but not all of them are necessarily useful to new managers. In addition, these metrics are of varying degrees of importance based on the industry or sector (private, public or non-profit) an organization falls into. For our purposes we are only going to discuss those ratios which are useful for both managers in general and new managers in particular.

Financial Health or "Liquidity"

Before we begin to review these types of measures in detail it is necessary to introduce an additional concept into our understanding of the Balance Sheet. In our simple example in the previous lesson we did not differentiate between those assets and liabilities which are considered short term versus those which are considered long term. Short-term assets are those which can be converted to cash fairly quickly (usually considered to be within the current accounting period). Short-term assets would include items like Cash on Hand, Accounts Receivable, Inventory, etc. Any of these non-cash assets are relatively easy to convert to cash, hence their classification as "current". Assets which are really more of a long term nature are referred to as Fixed Assets and include items such as Plant & Equipment, Land, etc., all items which are not easily converted to cash. Similarly, current liabilities refer to those obligations which are required to be settled in the near term, such as Accounts Payable, taxes payable, etc. Long term liabilities are, not surprisingly, obligations that stretch far beyond the current accounting period before they must be settled. The best example of this is a mortgage loan.

Measures about the financial health of an organization (often referred to as the "liquidity") serve a number of purposes. First, they help managers to understand the overall ability of the organization to survive in the short term. Second, they provide external sources of funding or suppliers (e.g., vendors, banks, investors, etc.) a picture of how risky it might be to extend credit to the organization.

The easiest of these ratios to produce and understand is the Current Ratio. The Current Ratio is so named because it reflects the ability of the organization to pay its current debts (lines of credit, vendor invoices, etc.) by using its current assets (those which can easily be converted into cash). The ratio is derived from the Balance Sheet via a straightforward mathematical equation:

Current Ratio = Current Assets / Current Liabilities

Assets				
	Current Assets			
	Cash on Hand	$	50,000	
	Accounts Receivable	$	80,000	
	Inventory	$	40,000	
	Total Current Assets			$ 170,000
	Fixed Assets			
	Plant, Building & Equipment	$	500,000	
	Total Fixed Assets			$ 500,000
	Total Assets			$ 670,000
Liabilities				
	Current Liabilities			
	Accounts Payable	$	40,000	
	Total Current Liabilities			$ 40,000
	Long Term Liabilities			
	Mortgage Payable	$	380,000	
	Total Long Term Liabilities			$ 380,000
Equity				
	Retained Earnings	$	100,000	
	Shareholder Equity	$	150,000	
	Total Equity			$ 250,000
	Total Liabilities & Equity			$ 670,000

Current Ratio = $170,000 / $40,000 = 4.25

So what does this really mean to managers? The Current Ratio in our example is suggesting that the organization has more than 4 times the available assets required to settle current debts. As a banker or vendor this means that there is likely low risk associated with extending credit to the organization so it would not be difficult to lend the organization money to fund growth. Viewed from the perspective of management, however, this might be telling them that they have assets which are underperforming – meaning that they aren't deriving as much value from them as they could. They should consider what alternatives they have to keeping cash in the bank that would provide better return on the cash asset (e.g., CDs or other investments).

The next measure of organizational financial health that new managers should be aware of is the Quick Ratio. The Quick Ratio is very similar to the Current Ratio except that it takes into account the likelihood that Inventory would actually take longer to convert to cash than other types of Current Assets. By deducting Inventory from the Current Ratio equation the resulting ratio is a more realistic measure of the ability of the organization to meet its obligations quickly.

Quick Ratio = (Current Assets – Inventory) / Current Liabilities

Assets				
	Current Assets			
		Cash on Hand	$ 50,000	
		Accounts Receivable	$ 80,000	
		Inventory	$ 40,000	
		Total Current Assets		$ 170,000
	Fixed Assets			
		Plant, Building & Equipment	$ 500,000	
		Total Fixed Assets		$ 500,000
	Total Assets			$ 670,000
Liabilities				
	Current Liabilities			
		Accounts Payable	$ 40,000	
		Total Current Liabilities		$ 40,000
	Long Term Liabilities			
		Mortgage Payable	$ 380,000	
		Total Long Term Liabilities		$ 380,000
Equity				
		Retained Earnings	$ 100,000	
		Shareholder Equity	$ 150,000	
		Total Equity		$ 250,000
	Total Liabilities & Equity			$ 670,000

Quick Ratio = ($170,000-$40,000) / $40,000 = 3.25

If the Quick Ratio is equal to or greater than 1, the organization is considered to be well situated to handle its debt. If, however, the Quick Ratio is less than 1 (which could easily occur if the cash on hand is actually coming from some form of current liability, such as a short term loan) the organization may experience difficulty meeting immediate obligations.

The last of the measures we will discuss is called Days Sales Outstanding (DSO for short). DSO tells us how long it usually takes for credit sales (Accounts Receivable) to be collected from customers. The equation for this metric looks like this:

Days Sales Outstanding = Accounts Receivable / (Credit Sales / Days)

Revenue				Assets			
	Sales	$	100,000		Current Assets		
					Cash on Hand $	50,000	
Expenses					Accounts Receivable $	80,000	
	Raw Materials	$	50,000		Inventory $	40,000	
	Salaries	$	25,000		*Total Current Assets*		$ 170,000
	Rent	$	12,000		Fixed Assets		
	Utilities	$	6,000		Plant, Building & Equipment $	500,000	
	Total Expenses	$	93,000		*Total Fixed Assets*		$ 500,000
					Total Assets		$ 670,000
	Profit (Loss)	$	7,000				

The additional piece of information necessary to compute DSO is the average revenue per business day during the accounting period in question. This is derived from the total sales figure reported on the Income Statement. For absolute precision this must be calculated with the actual number of days in each period (28, 30 or 31); however, it is sufficient for our purposes to use a figure of 30 days to represent the days in the accounting period being analyzed. Thus, the DSO calculation is as follows:

Days Sales Outstanding = $80,000 / ($100,000 / 30) = 24

This formula is telling us that, on average, the customers pay us within 24 days of the date of the sale. How would this be important to new managers? For one thing it tells managers when to expect the cash that results from sales. This is vital information to understand how cash flows in and out of the business (as we discussed in the previous chapter). Secondly, DSO tells managers whether the organization is effectively enforcing its collection policy. If the DSO is excessively long (45+ days) it would indicate that no process is being followed to resolve accounts receivable. In other words, you are losing the use of the money you are owed. That impacts profits by limiting the amount of cash available to fund growth in order to generate even greater profits.

Profitability

Speaking of profits, there are two fundamental profit metrics that provide critical information for managers. Profit is divided into two categories: Gross Profit and Net Profit. Gross Profit is that amount of money which is left over after the costs to actually produce the item sold are deducted. These production costs are referred to as Cost of Goods Sold. After all other expenses are deducted (light, heat, water, etc.) the resulting profit is the Net Profit. Gross Profit Margin is simply the Gross Profit restated as a percentage of total sales.

Gross Profit Margin = Gross Profit / Sales

Revenue		
	Sales $	100,000
Expenses		
	Raw Materials $	50,000
	Salaries $	25,000
	Rent $	12,000
	Utilities $	6,000
	Total Expenses $	93,000
	Profit (Loss) $	7,000

Gross Profit Margin = $25,000 / $100,000 = .25 or 25%

Similarly, Net Profit Margin is the percentage of total sales that the net profit represents.

Net Profit Margin = Net Profit / Sales
Net Profit Margin = $7,000 / $100,000 = .07 or 7%

As these two basic formulas indicate, it is possible to calculate individual Costs per Sales for each of the component expenses tracked on the Income Statement. Merely substitute the gross or net profit dollar amount with the amount of the individual expense to determine the percentage of sales that each expense consumes.

Financial Leverage
Financial Leverage is best described as the ability of the organization to "leverage" or utilize various sources of funding to stimulate profits. There are two primary measures of financial leverage with which managers are concerned. The first is called Return on Assets (ROA). ROA describes how efficiently the organization is using its own assets to generate profits. As you may have realized, this metric is derived from combining Income Statement data with Balance Sheet data (much like Days Sales Outstanding) in order to conduct the analysis.

Return on Assets = Net Profit (Annualized) / Total Assets
Using the annual Net Profit instead of only that from a single accounting period will provide a more meaningful measure. Therefore, we will assume that our example Income Statement reflects an accounting period equal to one month and that the Net Profit of $7,000 is roughly the same each month.

Return on Assets = ($7,000 x 12) / $670,000 = .125 = 12.5%
If you think about what this number represents—the efficiency with which the organization utilizes its assets—it stands to reason that the higher the ROA, the better managed the organization.

The second measure of financial leverage is the Debt-to-Equity Ratio. The Debt-To-Equity ratio compares how the organization is utilizing the equity provided by the owners (or shareholders) against the equity provided from borrowing. There is not really a "perfect" or "correct" ratio for this measure. It will vary with each organization. The Debt-To-Equity Ratio helps us to understand whether the organization is generally relying on its assets

Assets			
	Current Assets		
	Cash on Hand	$ 50,000	
	Accounts Receivable	$ 80,000	
	Inventory	$ 40,000	
	Total Current Assets		$ 170,000
	Fixed Assets		
	Plant, Building & Equipment	$ 500,000	
	Total Fixed Assets		$ 500,000
	Total Assets		$ 670,000
Liabilities			
	Current Liabilities		
	Accounts Payable	$ 40,000	
	Total Current Liabilities		$ 40,000
	Long Term Liabilities		
	Mortgage Payable	$ 380,000	
	Total Long Term Liabilities		$ 380,000
Equity			
	Retained Earnings	$ 100,000	
	Shareholder Equity	$ 150,000	
	Total Equity		$ 250,000
	Total Liabilities & Equity		$ 670,000

derived from ownership investment to grow profits or whether it relies more heavily on debt financing to fund growth. The formula is straightforward:

Debt-To-Equity Ratio = Total Debt / Total Equity
Debt-To-Equity Ratio = $420,000 / $250,000 = 1.68 or 168%

This example pertains to an organization that has chosen to finance its growth primarily by external debt rather than from its own ownership equity. Another way of describing this reliance on debt is to say that the organization is "highly leveraged." Is this a bad thing? It depends on the organization. If the firm does not generate enough cash in a given period it will find the burden of the heavy debt load to be difficult to sustain. If the debt instruments are interest rate sensitive (that is, they can fluctuate rates based on market conditions), the firm could take a serious cash hit in times when rates are higher.

Conversely, a firm that utilizes debt financing to grow is maximizing the assets of others to achieve their objectives. As long as the increased profits exceed the cost of the debt, then there is not anything inherently wrong with the approach. This frees a firm's own assets/equity to be used for other purposes.

Productivity

Productivity measures are simple to calculate but extremely useful for a manager to have available. There are several simple equations to consider:

- Backlog: Backlog represents the amount of firm orders received minus those orders which have already been shipped and billed. This can be represented as a number (i.e. the number of orders in backlog) or as dollars (i.e. the value of orders yet to be filled). Over time, a falling backlog measure indicates that Sales is not being successful in keeping the "pipeline" active, the result of which will be poor financial performance.
- Sales per Customer: As the name implies, this is a simple calculation of either the number of or value of the sales on a per customer basis. This is intended to be shown as an average rather than accurate to each specific customer. A rising trend in this measure indicates that the organization is selling larger amounts of products and services to existing customers, often referred to as cross-sell. If this measure is falling while the number of customers is remaining stagnant, the implication is that customers are buying less of what the organization has to offer. This may be because they are no longer loyal to the organization or that the mix of products offered is no longer in synch with what the marketplace wants. If it is falling while the number of customers is increasing it might be indicating that the average sale is getting smaller (either by small purchases or because of lower prices). In either case, managers need to understand what is happening in their customer base.
- Sales per Employee: Again, a simple metric to derive, yet it provides a wealth of information for the managers of an organization. This measure is an uncomplicated means of

determining how efficiently your labor force is being leveraged to generate sales. If Sales per Employee are rising, it means that the level of productivity of each employee is increasing and the firm is doing more with the same (or fewer) resources. This is a good condition to have as long as it is closely monitored. At some point the labor force will reach its maximum productivity and the only way to achieve higher sales is to expand the pool of workers. Doing so will immediately reduce the Sales per Employee metric back to a sustainable level (until the proverbial wall is once again hit).

- Sales per Square Foot: This metric is not universally useful, but it can be valuable when managers are analyzing the productive use of the organization's occupied space. Once again, an increasing rate indicates higher and higher rates of productivity out of the available space. Also once again there is a limit to the ability of the organization to generate sales from existing manufacturing, retailing or back office property. A simple example would be that of a restaurant that is constantly busy in the evening, with a consistently long wait time for customers to get a table. This is a great indication of maximum productivity being achieved from the available number of tables and production capacity of the kitchen. What it also suggests, however, is that any future growth will have to be the result of expanding facilities beyond their current capacity either by opening another restaurant or adding a new dining room, etc.

It Is All In the Numbers

Understanding management economics is at once one of the most difficult skills for new managers to master as well as one of the most critical. Managers cannot operate effectively on instinct alone. They require the balance of historical reporting on their overall performance and that of the organization as a whole. There is an old adage that goes "you cannot manage what you cannot measure." There is a great deal of wisdom in that phrase, despite the fact that it leaves out the human dimensions of management entirely. Surely, though, being able to measure organizational activity and then use that data to refine performance is at the core of management itself.

One note of caution: Management economics is most meaningful when viewed in the context of multiple time periods, whether multiple years, quarters or months. A snapshot of economic vitality can be deceiving if it is not part of a "big picture" analysis. In other words, remember to take a long view when acting on the numbers.

Financial Ratio Quick Reference
- *Current Ratio* The ability of the organization to pay its current debts out of its current assets.
- Quick Ratio The ability of the organization to pay its current debt out of its current assets, minus the value of any inventory (which is harder to convert to cash)
- Days Sales Outstanding The numbers of days that pass before customers typically pay their invoices.
- *Gross Profit (Margin)* That which left after deducting raw production costs from total revenue (sales).
- *Net Profit (Margin)* That which is left after deducting all expenses not related directly to production from gross profit.
- Return on Assets The efficiency with which the organization is using its assets to generate profits.
- Debt-To-Equity Ratio The comparison of how well the organization is using debt financing to grow versus using the accumulated equity of the owners (shareholders).
- *Backlog* The amount of firm orders received minus those orders already shipped and billed.
- Sales Per Customer Total sales divided by number of customers.
- Sales Per Employee Total sales divided by number of employees.
- Sales Per Square Foot Total sales divided by amount of square footage the organization occupies.

(The ratios in italics are those which are the most valuable to department managers. The remainder is occasionally used in specialized types of analysis.)

Motivating Your People

"If you must have motivation, think of your paycheck on Friday." -- Noel Coward, Actor, Director & Playwright

Getting the Most and the Best

Noel Coward is said to have spoken these words to actors, presumably because they were seeking his directorial guidance for how to play a particular role or recite some snippet of dialogue. Coward uttered this phrase many years before the rise of such peculiar tools of motivation such as office foosball, tank tops and flip flops as acceptable working clothes or employee coffee bars with espresso and soy lattes. Despite these modern contrivances of management, Coward's snide response is, unfortunately, all too often emblematic of the sort of thinking that new managers sometimes employ when trying to motivate their direct reports.

So what does it take to get the most out of human capital? The answer is that there is no single answer. Human beings are motivated by different ambitions, personal tastes and physical and emotional needs. At the most basic level, every human being is driven by fundamental needs for survival: food, water, shelter, etc. These simple demands form the basis of what famous psychologist Abraham Maslow referred to as The Hierarchy of

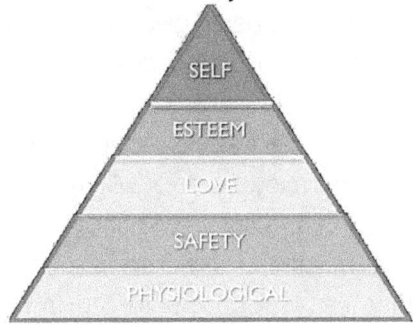

Needs. Maslow's theory is most frequently represented as a triangle; with those basic physiological needs previously mentioned serving as the

foundation of all other human need. Next comes the need for safety and security (whether physical, economic or emotional), then social needs, then esteem needs and lastly what are called self-actualization needs— those which make up the character of the individual. As each of the various levels of need is met, the focus of the person moves on to the next tier. The absence of needs being met is what provides motivation.

Where are most employees in the Maslow pyramid? Again, it will be different with every individual. It is likely that most of an organization's employees have, at minimum, most of their physiological and safety needs met (there are always exceptions, of course). Typically it is the third level of needs—the social needs—where most new managers will find their staff. Everything from this level and above is fair game for a leader to try to exploit in order to successfully motivate the workforce. It is not difficult to surmise that this leaves a great deal of latitude (some might say, ambiguity) when deciding how to motivate each person to achieve their best and their most.

Maslow's hierarchy is a useful guide for managers, but it is not a detailed roadmap to happier employees. At best, new managers would do well to acquire a solid understanding of the pyramid in order to broaden their general insights into what makes people "tick." For example, by accepting the notion that esteem needs are largely in play when employees performance review is being given, new managers can better prepare both their positive and not-so-positive remarks in order to elicit the desired response from the subject. How much will positive comments reinforce the individual's sense of confidence and self-esteem (and how much is too much)? How severely will the individual's sense of self-worth be damaged by biting criticism? Because there is no magic formula for getting the most and the best out of employees, new managers must shoulder the responsibility for striking the right balance in both good and bad performance reviews. It shouldn't be merely an exercise used for the sole purpose of letting employees know what their next raise will be.

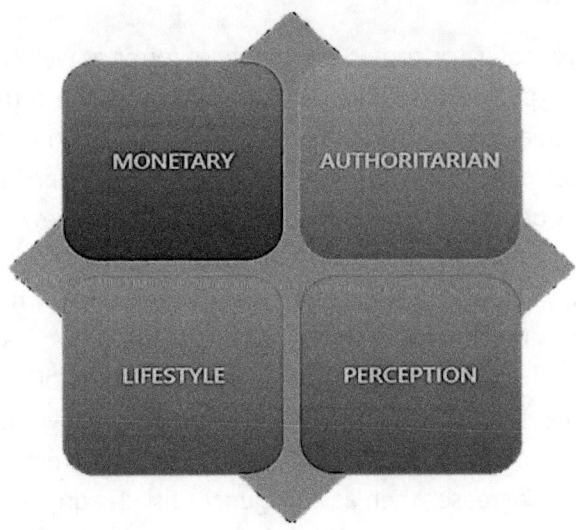

While a great many theories and psychological models have been developed on the subject of motivation, it is possible to narrow the wide range of options into a few different fundamental approaches. These are not scientific. In fact, they are anecdotal, based on personal observation of how individuals respond to various forms of motivation.

These motivational approaches fall into four categories: *Monetary, Authoritarian, Perception and Lifestyle*. Each of these has positive and negative characteristics to them, as one might expect. However, they have worked effectively when correctly used with the right employee.

Monetary
Motivating employees with money is perhaps the most used and most relied upon method. Some surveys peg the overall percentage of employees who respond positively to financial incentives at 54% while others claim it to be closer to 75-80%. Regardless of the precise number, the net take away is that money works as a motivator for some, if not most, people in the workforce. Differing demographic factors related to employees such as gender, age, education level, marital status and

"presence of children" play a role in shaping the actual responses to money of individuals.

The monetary motivator comes in a variety of forms as well. Perhaps the most widely expected is the annual raise. Whether the organization is white collar, blue collar or some mix of the two, there can be no denying that a performance review—generally conducted annually—is the perceived trigger for increasing base pay. This is viewed by some employees as a right rather than a privilege. Certainly that is true where collective bargaining agreements have been entered into which spell out exactly how much and when an increase in base pay is implemented. Historically this was accepted as a hard-fought "right" by the labor force. Increasingly, however, the use of incentives is beginning to find its way into contract negotiations—if not as a direct replacement for guaranteed increases then as an adjunct to such agreements.

In executive offices and even lower level management tiers, the use of money as a motivator is well established. Many white collar (or "professional") jobs have their compensation tied directly to performance. Not only are extra-salary options like bonuses based on individual, group or organizational performance, but typically employees in professional roles do not have any sort of guaranteed annual increase. In these cases money is usually more effective as a motivator because there is less of a sense of "entitlement" tied to it.

Whether the money factor involves base pay or bonuses or both, it is clear that, for a great many employees, it is a significant motivator. It is important to remember that not everyone is so inclined. Those who may have their financial security needs met through the income of a spouse or as a result of previous employment (think of all of the Silicon Valley millionaires created by the Dot Com revolution), new managers should be careful not to assume that throwing money at employees is always going to get them motivated to perform at their best.

Authoritarian

Authoritarian motivation is just what the name implies: the use of authority as a means of eliciting a desired response or behavior. This approach has all sorts of negative connotations associated with it, especially if viewed in the light of the types of power-centric new managers that are often encountered. Authoritarian management is not, however, about "throwing your weight around." It is rather the ability to judiciously apply the authority granted a manager to influence employees to do what is necessary and, indeed, to exceed minimum requirements.

The use of authority is not always about repercussions either. Frequently it is enough for employees to understand merely that managers have the ability to use their authority that stimulates expected performance. The famous maxim "Speak softly and carry a big stick" is the best interpretation of this model. Everybody knows managers have the big stick (the authority of their position) but most managers do not find it necessary to wield it like a baseball bat because employees also know that it will be used if necessary. Some might call this fear or intimidation. A better term might be "inevitable response"—the sure knowledge that failure to live up to norms and expectations will generate the inevitable response of authoritarian consequence.

For new managers this approach has a few shortcomings. First, most new managers will not enjoy the immediate respect of all of their employees. It must be earned over time. Consequently, the inevitable response concept is less effective because no one really knows how new leaders will respond to challenges to their authority. It is an unfortunate reality that, at some point (likely early in their tenure) new managers will be required to respond in authoritarian manner to a given situation. Under the best circumstances, the event is non-destructive to productivity and morale while conveying that the necessary action will occur, if provoked. Under the worst-case scenario new managers get their point across but at the expense of trust and respect from the workforce. These types of occasions make it difficult for managers to build the necessary bonds with the staff that enable them to withhold the "big stick" response.

Second, new managers are sometimes reluctant to use the authority granted them, particularly if they have been promoted from within. These managers tend to be careful not to upset friends and former co-workers by being "too bossy" or harsh. This is just as dangerous a precedent to set as acting too swiftly would be. It broadcasts a message to the staff (friend and foe alike) that the limits of acceptable performance are somehow wider or less defined than before. Given the opportunity to spot a weakness, employees may be tempted to try to derive as much leverage for themselves as possible. This will prove extraordinarily troublesome for managers down the line, not only from those whose cooperation was always in question but also from those allies they may have among the labor pool. Knowing when to act with authoritarian force and in what proportion is the sort of tightrope walk that paralyzes many new managers. Time and experience are the best teachers, but awareness of the potential for disaster is a critical success factor for the here and now.

Perception

This category of motivation is difficult to quantify because it is so closely tied to the individual egos of those involved. As we've seen, many employees are incented by money and still others by authority. It is hard to know with any certainty how many are motivated by how they are perceived among their peers and by their supervisor(s). This issue is that which is best reflected by Maslow's esteem needs level in the hierarchy of needs.

A manager can use perception (or, how employees see themselves and how others view them) as a motivator but only with limited effect. The types of actions which might be seen under this approach are the granting of a particular job title, the movement from cube to office (or, at least, a bigger and better positioned cube), the assignment of a preferred parking place, etc. These are sometimes known as "perks" and, while they may have some intrinsic value unto themselves, more often than not they are real value is in how employees perceive their status among their peers when they receive them. If managers know of individuals who are sensitive to the perceptions they have of themselves and how others perceive them, it is entirely possible (and ethical) to use the awarding of perks as a motivator, especially in combination with a more conservative use of the monetary approach. So it is possible to blend both a modest compensation incentive with a perception-based benefit to stimulate the desired behavior or performance from employees.

There are times when this is a bit risky. It is very easy to "train" employees that title expansion and other sorts of perception perks come more easily than money. A successful small business owner once remarked that "Titles are only of use to you if you are looking for a job," meaning that the only audiences who may be impressed with fancy titles are those with whom you do not already work. Title creep and office creep and all of the other ego-driven motivators can quickly move from productive to destructive, especially if they become an expectation of the workforce. This can happen quite quickly in an organization where direct compensation is under pressure due to poor financial performance. New managers, especially, want to avoid any and all friction as a result of smaller (or even non-existent) raises, so they reach for the "free" bonus to soothe the hurt feelings of their employee(s). Just like money, however, an attitude of entitlement can evolve that causes more problems than simply saying "no" initially might have done.

Lifestyle

Lifestyle motivators are among the most effective and personally satisfying tools that managers can employ. These incentives are basically highly targeted solutions to employees motivation concern that take into account the wants, needs and desires of the individual in ways not addressed by the motivational approaches of Monetary, Authoritarian or Perception. They are effective because they answer specific needs for specific individuals rather than force-fitting them into a "one size fits all" approach. Lifestyle incentives are not simple to identify and even more challenging to implement because they require that managers know their staff well enough to understand what they enjoy, what their family enjoys, what triggers their intellectual curiosity and so on. Not all managers have the ability or the willingness to develop the relationships with their employees that are required to answer these sorts of questions. But they really should.

Some examples of lifestyle incentives might include: a six game set of tickets to a professional sports team that the manager knows employees follows closely; season tickets to the symphony or membership in other cultural venues (like museums, zoos, etc.) where employees might take their whole family; permission for employees to take their "significant other" along on a business trip (perhaps combining a Thursday or Friday trip with an all-expense paid weekend). These may seem frivolous or in some cases even extravagant, but in the larger scheme these sorts of motivators are enormously powerful because they say two things directly to employees: "I know you well enough to know what you like and I care enough about you to spend the time to think about something unique and personalized for you." These small touches exceed the limits of the employer/employee relationship to actively demonstrate concern and interest in employee's immediate family and friends. It is seldom that such proactive thinking is met with cynicism or derision.

Smaller organizations have greater freedom to implement a program of lifestyle motivators than most large organizations. This is because small groups can more directly control how widespread the use of such incentives grows to be. Larger concerns would find it problematic to manage such an unstructured program, although it is possible to do so even when there is a large employee population. The secret to succeeding with this motivational approach is to follow the Ritz-Carlton model.

The Ritz-Carlton hotel chain is among the world's most prestigious and luxurious. It is also, by consequence, one of the most expensive. The management of the Ritz-Carlton know what makes them different is their commitment to customer service that exceeds all expectations. In order to guarantee that such service levels are consistently met (in other words, to institutionalize the service culture), one of the programs now made legendary is that the hotel grants employees the ability to spend up to $2000 per guest per day to fix any problem experienced by the guest. Because senior management knows that the key differentiator to the loyalty of guests is how they are treated when things go wrong as much as when they go right, this investment pays off handsomely by the fact that the average Ritz-Carlton customer will spend an average of $250,000 with the firm over their lifetime.

Could such a model work in an organization seeking to motivate its employees rather than customers? Could managers be given an annual budget for lifestyle incentives that is used at their discretion to reward exemplary performance? Indeed this can work if the organization trusts the management team to effectively manage the potential for abuse that such an approach could entail.

Effective Motivation Does Not Come In Standard Sizes

STRENGTHS
- Tech savvy
- Social media savvy
- More educated
- Dedicated to shared value systems
- More tolerant of social diversity

WEAKNESSES
- Short attention span
- Different work ethic
- No loyalty to organization
- Attitude of entitlement
- Motivated to perform but only at a price

OPPORTUNITIES
- Creative approaches to problem solving
- Work-life balance leads to productivity improvements
- Fulfilled/healthier team reduces healthcare burden

THREATS
- Inescapable future talent pool
- Increased turnover rates & recruitment costs
- Increased training costs
- Potential for loss of institutional knowledge

Motivating human beings can be a complex equation, if allowed to become one. Alternatively, it can be simply and straightforwardly developed based on the experience, values, commitment and creativity of the managers who lead. Just as no two people are built exactly the same way, with the same proportions and hair color and likes and dislikes, so too should no two motivational models be expected to work across the board. Organizations are made up of living beings, not computer models or behavioral studies or psychological theory. People respond best to those stimulants that address their specific needs, whether they are basic issues like financial security, or lifestyle matters that go directly to their wellbeing and that of their families. Authority, too, can be an effective tool for motivating employees, provided it is used judiciously and with a grander plan in mind.

Looking Ahead

Motivation practices are changing because the workforce is changing. The traits of the "Millennial" generation are making long held views passé. The SWOT diagram at left details some of the typical values and behaviors that are hallmarks of this new labor force. Savvy managers are already working with HR to develop employee motivators that have the best chance to be successful.

Management Presentation Skills

"We cannot make good news out of bad practice." Edward R. Murrow, Journalist

Getting the Message Across

An often overlooked aspect of management is the requirement for managers to make regular presentations of organizational "news" to a variety of audiences. Sometimes the news can be good, such as to announce a new product or report on a successful operating period. Sometimes the news is not good at all, such as when it must be reported that a new product will be late to market. The audiences for this information can include clients, coworkers, senior executives, Boards of Directors, trade show attendees, etc. As different as managing is from just about any other frontline mission, so too is making presentations frequently a major challenge for new managers. Yet getting the message across through such presentations is a critical task for all managers.

The First Challenge: Stage Fright

For many new managers unaccustomed to speaking in front of an audience, giving a presentation can be terrifying. The term "stage fright" is often used to identify the nervous stomach and quivering hands many novice speakers must contend with. While growing up we may have been taught to try to imagine the audience is sitting in their underwear, supposedly because it will allow us to view them in a non-threatening light. Such tactics may be OK to explain to a ten-year-old making a book report, but they are useless to new managers facing an audience of their peers for the first time. It may seem unfeeling to say so, but stage fright is truly nothing more than a poor excuse used by new managers for not knowing their material. It is certainly true that some people are so naturally insecure that they would have trouble speaking in front of any group, large or small, whether they were strangers or intimate friends. Such cases are the exception, rather than the rule. For most of us, it comes down to insecurity driven by a lack of adequate preparation or less than total confidence in the material we are presenting. Stage fright is really in our hands to control.

It may help to think of the situation this way: When we are engaged in casual conversation with friends or family, talking about our jobs or what the kids did last night, we are usually totally at ease and can speak confidently and animatedly with great authority. We can do so because we know the subject inside and out. We are convinced that no one in the room at that time can possibly know the material we are discussing any better than we do.

Giving a management presentation should be viewed in the same way. There is nothing redeemable about new managers attempting to present important news, facts or figures that they are either unfamiliar with or unprepared to discuss in greater detail. This might seem a rather simple concept to accept: however every day countless managers stand up to speak or lead a discussion on a topic about which they are truly unqualified. This is no one's fault but the speaker's.

The solution to stage fright borne out of informational insecurity is preparation. There can be no substitute for it. Preparation demands that speakers make the material a part of their own "reservoir of experience" from which they can call up whatever supporting arguments may be necessary to get the message across. This may be in the form of persuasive logic or detailed statistics. Granted, memorizing facts and figures is a bit like trying to memorize the state capitols when we were children and novice presenters can easily get distracted trying to instantaneously recall such data. In such cases, it is acceptable and well-advised to have the benefit of slides or charts or some other form of visual aid that display complex information in a cogent manner. This requires that the presenter spends sufficient time in collecting and organizing the data to be reviewed to be able to speak about it in depth without having to read it verbatim from a typewritten page, because there is nothing more insulting to an audience than to be read, word for word, the content of a slide or chart.

Regardless of the topic or the level of knowledge speakers may have prior to making their presentation, by the time they must get in front of an audience they must know the material to be presented intimately. Furthermore, the audience is granting the speaker exclusive use of their time, for however long it takes, to present their information, arguments and ideas. At all times throughout a presentation, speakers must demonstrate respect for the audience by not belittling them and by avoiding the striking of an attitude of condescension. Just because speakers may be considered the "experts," it does not give them the right to arrogantly remind the audience of their prowess. Humility must be the watchword throughout.

The Second Challenge: Constructing the Presentation

There is no better time for speakers to get to know their topic well than when they set out to organize the material into an effective presentation, because it is the organization of the speech that initially determines how successful the speaker will be. Whether the presentation is prepared using tools like Microsoft PowerPoint or Excel or merely reinforced by flip charts or photo slideshows, the order and path through which presenters takes their audience will, in large measure, impact how persuasive or informative the event turns out to be.[6]

To aid in this organizational process there is a "golden rule" of public speaking that states "You tell them what you are going to tell them, you tell them and then you tell them what you just told them." In other words, every presentation must have a beginning, middle and end that continually restate the purpose and content of the subject.

We can easily break down these various stages into outline form:

Opening: Tell them what you are going to tell them

- *Bold Statement:* Begin the presentation with a bold statement or provocative idea that will immediately engage the audience. Saying something like "Stage fright is a poor excuse for not knowing the material" may seem harsh, but it is guaranteed to get the audience's attention because it will strike a chord with those who have struggled with stage fright. Not every bold statement must be borderline inflammatory. It is sometimes sufficient to simply state an alarming fact or recite a famous and particularly appropriate quote.

- *Humorous Short Story:* If you are comfortable enough to tell a short, amusing story it can break down whatever artificial barriers that may exist between the speaker and the audience. This does not necessarily have to be related to the topic, but be careful not to tell a story that may seem funny to you but which could be offensive to certain audience members.

- *Present a Contradiction:* You might choose to open with a statement such as "Despite the fact that home computers and the Internet have increased access to the world's knowledge, overall school test scores have been decreasing for the last ten years." The contradiction seeks to identify something which is exactly the opposite of what one might expect to find.

- *Summarize the Topic:* This is a must, regardless of which of the openings you choose to use. Once the joke or contradiction has been put before the audience, it is the speaker's responsibility to summarize for them what they are about to hear. The key to this is to not go too deeply into the actual material about to be presented. Merely give the highlights of the information that will be discussed. This can be aided by a slide with a meeting agenda on it, if the situation warrants it.

Body: Tell them

- *Know Your Material COLD:* As has already been stated, this is an absolute for any management presentation (or any speech in general).

- *Work from an Outline, Not a Script:* Because an outline forces speakers to actually form sentences on the fly, the effect can be either a powerful statement of absolute authority on a given topic. However, if the author is not sufficiently prepared, it can expose speakers to serious doubt about their knowledge and command of the facts. Which of those actually results is purely in the control of presenters.

- *Stick to the Highlights (Unless Detail Is Required):* A common mistake many new managers make in preparing business presentations is believing that they must get every thought or idea or event into their material. It is not necessary to provide endless examples to support an argument so keep them limited to one or two that best represent the point trying to be made. "Stay out of the weeds" if possible, meaning do not get mired in facts and figures that confuse, rather than illustrate, the statements you make. If detail is required (as might be the case in an engineering presentation), be certain to accurately judge the ability of the majority of the audience to comprehend the information.

- *Weave The Story Together Through Segues):* When moving from one subject or argument to another, transition between ideas eases the audience into the new material, tying that which has already been presented to that which is about to be discussed. In the entertainment industry this is referred to as a *segue* (to make a transition from one thing to another smoothly and without interruption: ⫫

- *Using Visual Aids:* Visual aids should enrich a presentation, not serve as a replacement for expert content, unless it is an illustration so dramatic that no words are necessary for the audience to comprehend its meaning. Projected material, such as PowerPoint slides are useful but require the use of technology that might not work. Another tactic is to pass visual aids from audience member to audience member or provide each with a copy. Again, caution is advised, because listeners will definitely be distracted as they focus their attention on the item in their hands and away from the presenter. Such visual aids should be used sparingly unless they are necessary while presenting complex concepts/materials. Finally, avoid laser pointers which can damage eyes or distract listeners.

Closing: Tell them what you told them

- *Restate Your Main Point (Thesis):* Here, again, is the opportunity to make the point once more without it seeming to be browbeating. After all of the material supporting the main thesis has been presented, it is an opportune time to state again what the original point of the presentation was. This will bring listeners back to the highest level in the discussion and remind them of the original premise.

- *Review the Highlight:* Take listeners back over the arguments and examples already reviewed in order to help them reconnect the dots of your presentation. This serves as a gentle yet effective reminder of the points that have been made.
- *Close with "Class":* End the presentation with as much class and respect for the audience as can be mustered. Thank them for their time and attention, make a mildly self-deprecating joke (such as 'I'm glad I did not put you to sleep') and be gracious in thanking hosts, if appropriate. End with a thought provoking challenge to the audience that will force them to continue to think about the material after they have left the room.

Some Thoughts about Slide Content

Constructing the presentation in a logical and flowing manner is critical to speaking success. So, too, is deciding what to put into visual aids like PowerPoint slides, if they are used to support the discussion. A common mistake for new presenters is to fill the slide with full sentences in bullet form, as many to a page as can be squeezed in. No one will take the time to read these, so do not waste your time. If they did, they would only be distracted from what you were saying currently, forcing them to try to catch up. Keep bulleted lists terse and to the point. Dispense with flowery language and state what needs to be said. The audience will be able to fill in the sentence structure blanks so long as the main elements of the statement are present. Use graphics in a limited way to break up the monotony of the text—pictures or clip art or movie clips—the options are limited only by the imagination. Once again, however, be sensitive to the audience and the material. Do not select comic-book style clip art in order to be "cute" if the subject matter is of a serious nature. Judge the purpose of the presentation and then align the graphical augmentation with that purpose. The material presented should be what "news" is, not the presenter is themselves.

The Employment Lifecycle

"If a man has a talent and cannot use it, he has failed. If he has a talent and uses only half of it, he has partly failed. If he has a talent and learns somehow to use the whole of it, he has gloriously succeeded and won a satisfaction and a triumph few men ever know." Thomas Wolfe, Author

Hiring the Right People

Hiring right is one of the most important decisions you will make as a supervisor. A good hire can improve your department's productivity and achievements for years to come (and reflect well on you). On the other hand, the consequences of a bad hire can be significant. Diminished productivity, turnover costs and the expense of litigation can bring a company to its knees. So you need to actively manage the hiring process, insuring that you are making good investments with your future hires.

As a manager, you may have limited control over hiring because your human resources department may handle many of the hiring tasks. Whatever role you play, however, you need to have a good understanding of the basics of how to make a good hire. Hiring mistakes typically occur for one of two reasons: 1) failure to follow hiring practices consistent with state and federal laws, or 2) failure to follow good hiring practices because of a rush to fill a vacant position.

Discrimination

The biggest legal pitfall in hiring—and the one that could land your company in the hottest water—is illegal discrimination. Hiring is one area where you must be especially careful to not discriminate against people based on what is referred to as their *protected class*. It is illegal to base a hiring decision on discriminatory factors that are protected under federal, state or local laws. This includes race, color, sex, pregnancy, religion, national origin, citizenship, disability, age, union activity, military service, marital status (in some localities) and sexual orientation (in some localities). Here is a list of protected classes that you must ignore in making any employment decision:

- Race, color and national origin. You cannot discriminate against an applicant or employee because of their skin color, their race or their nationality. This means that you cannot refuse to hire candidates because they are African-American or because they are from Mexico. It also means that you cannot pick light-skinned African-Americans over darker-skinned African-Americans because of their skin color. That would be color discrimination.
- Religion. You cannot discriminate against applicants or employees because of their religion. If applicants come to your office and state they are atheists, you must overlook that in making your hiring decision, regardless of your personal convictions. The same applies if the person is Jewish, Muslim, Christian, etc.
- Sex or Gender. You cannot discriminate against applicants or employees because of their sex or gender. The meaning is obvious: You cannot pick a man over a woman based merely on the fact that he is a man. Neither can you refuse to hire a woman because she is pregnant or might get pregnant.
- Age. You cannot take a person's age into consideration when making your hiring decision if that person's age is 40 or above,
- Disability. You cannot discriminate against applicants or employees because of their disability or perceived disability. This means that you cannot take an applicant's physical or mental conditions into consideration unless it prevents them from performing the job. You also cannot consider workers' compensation histories.
- Veteran Status. You cannot discriminate against applicants because they are veterans.
- Union Status. You cannot discriminate against applicants or employees because of their membership in a union.

It is very important when you interview candidates that you do not ask them any questions that would cause them to give you information about these protected classes. For example, do not ask what church they go to or if they were injured in their previous job. Instead, keep the questions job-related. Ask whether they can work the assigned hours, such as on Sunday morning, or whether they have any problem lifting 25 pounds. That way you are asking questions that give you the information you need to make a good decision without finding out information that is defined as illegal or irrelevant.

The Hiring Process

Job openings come about in several different ways. A current employee resigns, or someone has been terminated, or perhaps you are creating a new position or adding additional staffing to a current job category. Regardless of how the position arose, the ball is now in your court and you bear the responsibility for getting the process right.

Job Description

Before you begin the hiring process, take a minute to review the position's job description. Having an accurate, detailed job description is crucial to making a good hire. After all, how can you choose the best candidate until you pinpoint what you are looking for? If the job description is out of date and hasn't been updated for some time, it is crucial that you revise it. Jobs tend to morph into altogether different positions as the core competencies of employees begin to drive their occupational reach. It is very important that you remove any outdated terms or requirements. For example, you should avoid having a job description laced with trendy or outdated terms like "straw man" or "typist." Here are the steps you can follow:

- Identify the essential functions of the job—the things that must be done by the person in this job
- Identify the critical skills, abilities and overall knowledge required for the position
- Identify the chain of command, both above and below the position
- List the working conditions, hours and travel requirements

- Describe the physical and mental requirements, such as using a computer, moving boxes, or interacting with customers
- State that the job includes any and all other duties as needed and directed by the supervisor
- Include employment status such as part-time or full-time

If you do not have a job description or are creating a new job, it is the perfect time to create a comprehensive job description. Follow the above steps to describe the job duties.

Using gender-neutral language when drafting job descriptions does not have to be awkward. The goal is to avoid using gender-exclusive terms, not to draw attention to your political-correctness. Avoid using "he/she" at all costs. The English language has only "he" and "she" for third person singular pronouns, but a simple tip is to use plural language instead of singular language. Instead of a job description that reads, "An employee should submit his timesheet before he leaves on Friday," it could read, "employees should submit their timesheets before they leave on Friday."

Interviewing

The interview is your best opportunity to discover enough information about applicants to decide whether they are the best fit for the job. Do not take interviews lightly. You likely won't get another chance to gather information or form an opinion about applicants. Do your homework before the interview. You should gather and review résumés, applications and work samples, if applicable. Once you have all of you materials, review them carefully. Look at the applicant's skills and experience. Make a note of specific items to ask the applicant about.

Interview Questions

Your organization may have a standard list of interview questions. If so, take a look at those questions and decide which ones are relevant to the job. For example, if you are hiring a bricklayer you probably do not need to ask what kind of advanced degree the applicant holds.

If you do not have a ready-made list of questions, you will need to put your own list together. The interview will go much better if you think of the questions ahead of time. Furthermore, you should ask basically the same questions of all applicants so you do not inadvertently discriminate against one of them.

Below are some sample interview questions:

- What did you like best about your last/present job?
- What did you like least about your last/present job?
- Why are you leaving your current position?
- What attracts you to this job opening?
- What would your previous supervisor consider your biggest contribution to the company?
- What are your best skills and how would they best be put to use in this job?
- What makes you stand out among your peers? What do you want to avoid in your next job?
- What else is there about you and your skills that you would like me to know?

Behavioral Interviewing

Behavioral interviewing is a style of questioning that has become popular in recent years. Essentially, the interviewer asks questions about behavioral events or real-life situations, such as, "Tell me about a time when ... and how did you overcome that?" or "What would you do if...?" In this way applicants have to come up with a scenario and then apply their skills and judgment to the situation. You can tell a lot about an applicant by listening to how they have handled situations in the past.

Below are some sample behavioral interviewing questions:

- Describe a situation when you used persuasion to convince someone to see things your way
- Describe a time when you were faced with a stressful situation that demonstrated your coping skills
- Give me a specific example of a time when you used good judgment and logic in solving a problem
- Give me an example of a time when you set a goal and were able to meet or achieve it

[85]

- Tell me about a time when you had to use presentation skills to influence someone's opinion
- Give me a specific example of a time when you had to conform to a policy with which you did not agree

Questions to Avoid

You must exercise caution regarding the questions you ask applicants. You should not ask any questions that are designed to have applicants reveal any information about their membership in a protected class. While you may think you need to know certain information, asking about it may be illegal.

Here are some (but definitively not all) questions you definitely want to avoid in an employment interview. Although some of these questions may technically be legal to ask, they could be evidence that you are considering illegal factors in your hiring decision.

For example, if you innocently ask a foreign applicant where they are from and you do not hire them, they might think that their national origin was the reason why you rejected them. Steer clear of questions relating to

- Marital status or maiden name
- Children, pregnancy, or plans to have children
- Age or any questions that might reveal age
- Gender, race, national origin and any questions that might reveal these characteristics
- Arrests (convictions are okay)
- Citizenship, ancestry, accents, or place of birth
- Workers' compensation claims or work-related injuries
- Health, illnesses, injuries, or mental health
- Union membership
- Political membership or activities
- Church or religion

Measuring Ability to Do the Job

You may require applicants to take a test to determine whether they can do what they say they can do, such as typing or lifting. You can administer tests that aren't health-related without much worry; however, keep the following points in mind:

- Make sure all tests are job-related and justified by a legitimate business need
- Require the same tests of all applicants. For example, if you have an English test, do not just give it to foreign-sounding applicants
- Keep all test results confidential

If you are making up your own test, run it by HR or an employment law specialist to make sure it does not unintentionally discriminate against someone in a protected class.

Beware the ADA
The Americans with Disabilities Act (ADA) limits the health-related questions you can ask applicants and the tests you can have applicants perform. The time that you can ask for this information is critical. The dividing line is before you make a job offer and after you make a job offer.

Before the job offer you cannot ask anything about the health of applicants, such as whether they have any health problems, if they have ever been injured, or are they disabled. Applicants might have a hidden disability and need help doing the job, but they do not have to tell you until they are hired. Before the job offer you can ask

- Can you perform the essential functions of the job, with a reasonable accommodation if necessary?
- Please describe or demonstrate how you would perform the job's essential functions
- Can you meet the attendance requirements of the job?
- Do you have the required education and licenses to perform the job?

After the job offer you have more freedom in the questions you can ask and the tests you can require applicants to take. You may make an offer contingent on the results of medical and other tests designed to ensure that applicants can perform the job's essential functions without posing a direct threat to themselves or others.

A Final Decision

One of the hardest parts of hiring is making that final decision about the right candidate to hire. Sometimes the perfect candidate is obvious— someone with the right background, skills and personality to fit in with your company. But most of the time you will have to weigh different factors to come up with a decision. Here are some things to consider when weighing a candidate's strengths:

- Technical skills and experience
- Past job experience
- General knowledge of the field and the position
- Ability to learn new tasks

It is okay to use "intangibles" to judge candidates. These may include the candidate's personality, ability to fit into the company, or the candidate's commitment. You can even make your decision based on your "gut feeling" about a candidate. You need to make sure, however, that you are not using "personality" as a proxy for an illegal practice, such as race or sex discrimination. That is against the law.

Background Checks and References

Background and reference checks are a tricky area, so you should check with your HR department or an employment law specialist before going forward. Because of the confidential nature of information revealed during background checks, most companies have the HR department conduct the checks.

If you are responsible for performing reference and background checks, keep in mind that checking the references and background of applicants is a crucial step in the hiring process and one that you should not overlook under any circumstance. The types of reference and background checks that are allowed vary widely from state to state. Follow your state law and your company's policies, to make sure that you are taking the right steps. Your background check should consist of 1) a check of all listed references; 2) a check of recent former employers; and 3) a criminal background check if required by law or necessary for the job.

Making the Offer

An offer of employment must be made by the right person at the right time on the right terms. After you have concluded the search process and made a decision, you should extend an offer to the applicant. Be careful not to make any binding promises, such as "You will have a job as long as you do well." Lastly, do not oversell the job or the benefits. Instead, tell the applicant about the following terms:

- Job title
- Compensation and whether it is salaried or hourly with overtime
- Other critical job-specific items (e.g., location)
- Contingencies—limits on the length of the position, if known
- Primary benefits and the definitive source for additional information
- Conditions of employment

Conclusion

Keep foremost in your mind that the consequences of bad hiring can be significant. Hiring is an investment, so make sure you hone your skills and give your best effort to find a good fit for your company.

Documentation

Imagine this: It is the middle of a long, busy—not to mention stressful—day and you are wondering how you are going to meet the next deadline. Then you overhear one of your employees telling a dirty joke within earshot of your whole crew. This particular employee is violating your company's harassment policy and it is not his first time. You sternly tell him to knock it off and stop telling dirty jokes at work. He seems to get the message.

Are you done? You have the nagging feeling that you should fill out some sort of disciplinary form, especially since this is the second time you caught him telling dirty jokes. But you convince yourself that you do not have time to drop everything just to do paperwork. It is not that big a deal, right?

Actually, documentation *is* a really big deal. It protects you and your employer, creating proof that you are running your department the way you should. Basically, documentation is anything that is written down, such as these common documents:

- Performance evaluation
- Any type of memo
- Written warning
- Written documentation of a verbal warning
- HR and payroll forms
- Timecards and records
- Leave forms
- A notation of an award or promotion
- Any other employment-related document

Know Your Responsibility

As a supervisor, you've got your hands full keeping your employees on track. You may be tempted to wonder why you should be expected to fill out forms, write memos and struggle with performance evaluations when you are so busy tending to business. The answer to that question lies in the fact that your documentation can be the oil that keeps the organizational machine humming instead of breaking down at the worst possible time.

Because you are a manager or supervisor, you know better than most that problems come up in the workplace. You deal with everything from tardy or absent employees to allegations of discrimination, harassment, violence, or other kinds of mistreatment. No matter how well you handle those problems, your actions can be meaningless if there is nothing down in black and white to document that you've taken steps to solve problems and right wrongs. Employment lawyers generally tell supervisors, "If you do not have time to document properly, then you shouldn't be a supervisor". While that may seem harsh, the point is quite clear—make time for proper documentation.

Who Will Read This Stuff?

There are many situations when it is important that employee's personnel file has thorough, accurate documentation submitted by you. A few examples include

- If you want to fire someone for a long-term performance problem, your company probably will want to see documentation of the problem and your warnings to employees. Otherwise, you might not be allowed to fire them.
- A new supervisor may need your written record of employee's performance and conduct.
- When you are writing a performance evaluation, you should read last year's evaluation to help you judge what employee's done since then.
- If one of your employees ever sues your employer, then the lawyers, judge and jury will expect you to have written records to back up your story.

While poor documentation is fundamentally bad management, does it make you a lawbreaker? No, but it can make you look like one. Consider this sample scenario:

> You have to choose employees to lay off and you pick Brandi, a loudmouth with a bad attitude who is your slowest worker and makes a lot of mistakes. Unfortunately, you never wrote down these problems in her performance evaluations. She sues your company, saying she's a good worker. She claims the real reason you laid her off is illegal retaliation because she forcefully confronted the CEO about the company health insurance at a meeting last month. Now, instead of substantiating your justification for selecting her, you have to convince the court that the positive (or,

at least, non-negative) performance evaluations you gave her were inaccurate!

The point is that your records are often what make the difference between winning and losing an employment lawsuit. Of course, you hope disputes do not go all the way to the courtroom. Even if the company wins a case, just going to trial is expensive and distracting. Again, documentation is vital, because solid documentation of an employer's action can be instrumental in discouraging employees from filing lawsuits.

What Should You Write Down?
Here are some of the employment-related topics on which you are expected to keep records

- Hiring decisions
- Disciplinary matters
- Employee performance
- Promotions and commendations
- Demotion and termination decisions

Are these the sort of issues that prompt complaints? Absolutely! As a manager, you better have good reasons for choosing one job applicant over another. You better have the facts straight before meting out discipline; you know your employees deserve to know if they are meeting expectations on performance; likewise, you know you need to keep track of when and why employees are promoted, rewarded, demoted; and fired. Those are the kinds of issues that can make a rejected applicant, current employee or ex-employee angry enough to make trouble. But it is within the manager's power to stop someone bent on suing if you are careful to fully document every incident related to employees that falls within the broad terms listed above. If you've done the right thing—and usually you have—you can prove it through your documentation.

Other Reasons to Document

Keeping good records goes beyond staying out of legal trouble. It is part of your job to give your employees feedback that will keep them learning and improving. Performance evaluations may be the best form of documentation to aid employee development. A carefully written evaluation communicates to employees what they are doing right, what is not so right and what is expected in the area of improvement.

Disciplinary forms also are a type of feedback. For example, written warnings tell employees that they made a serious mistake, spell out what they need to do differently in the future and what will happen if they do not. By providing documentation in the form of performance evaluations and other kinds of written feedback, you are helping your employees to grow their own career. Often documentation is housed in employee's personnel file, but do not be fooled into thinking that if it is not in the file it does not count. If employees sue the company, the lawyers will demand to see *everything* that was ever written down about employees. That would include notes that are kept in a desk drawer (even if it is scribbled on a hamburger wrapper), work-related notes that a manager may keep at home, computer files and e-mail. All of these can find their way to the desk of a disgruntled employee's lawyer. The lawyer may even hire a computer expert to recover e-mail and computer files that have been deleted.

Forms, Forms, Forms

Filling out forms may be a tedious chore, but forms are a vital aspect of any documentation program. Forms make it easier to collect names, the date, the type of infraction, the action you are taking and the signatures of you and the offending employee. There will also likely be a space to describe the incident. That is where managers must get specific and tells the facts of what happened and why they took action. Managers should think in terms of what policies were violated, the effect of the infraction on the organization and whether employees have been disciplined for similar offenses previously.

Give Employees Their Say

The employer's evaluation forms and disciplinary forms may include a space where employees can write comments. That gives employees a chance to have their say (and it makes it hard for employees to change their story later). Even if the form does not have a space for employee comments, let them add them anyway, especially if they ask to. Encourage them do it immediately while in the office. Do not let them take it home or come back the next day.

Sign the Dotted Line

A vital part of any documentation is the signature section. It is important to make sure that you, as the supervisor, sign the form and that employees also sign. Your signature shows that you take responsibility for what is written and employees' signatures show that they saw the document, though not necessarily that the employee agrees with what you've written. If employees are reluctant to sign, let them know they are welcome to include their own comments for the file. If employees still won't sign, get a witness—another supervisor or someone from the HR department—to sign that the employee saw the document and refused to sign.

Mind Your Memos

Your employer may not have a form for every issue that requires documentation. In this case you need to write a memo. Some supervisors are intimidated without having a form to follow, but a memo will be easier if you stay focused and keep it simple. Remember the purpose: if writing a memo to document a performance issue, remember that the goal is to turn employees around. Be specific about what is wrong and about future expectations. Do not be cryptic in a written memo just because the situation has already been discussed with employees. Repeat in the memo what has been talked about before, that way the memo fully informs anyone reading it, even if it is years later.

Documentation Tips

- Keep it simple: A document is not much good if people cannot understand what has been written. The writing should be clear and simple. Do not struggle to be formal or fancy.
- Keep it brief: Just include what is important.
- Be thorough: Do not leave people guessing what is meant. Include times and dates. Include examples of the behavior or performance being written about. Include relevant policies and the effect of any violation on other employees or the organization's bottom line. Also include required changes employees is obligated to make and any deadlines imposed.
- Be timely: If the date on the documentation is days or weeks after the alleged infraction, it may leave a false impression that you did not take the matter seriously enough to spend ten or fifteen minutes to write it up, or even that you did not think the infraction was a problem until you had time to build up anger or resentment about it.

Know How Not To Document

Is *any* documentation better than nothing? No, there are times when bad documentation is worse than none at all. When working on documenting employees' actions, do not make any of these mistakes:

- Do not produce an illegible product: This includes everything from making sure the handwriting on forms is legible to making sure the narrative keeps to the point in memos. You are not communicating if your employees cannot read your sloppy scrawl. You are also not communicating if you ramble on to the extent that your employees do not know what you are trying to say. Think what a lawyer could make of careless, incoherent documentation.
- Do not forget signatures: Of course you will sign the document, but do not forget to have employees sign it too. Otherwise, it looks like you made up the whole incident, and employees never had any inkling that anything was wrong.

- Think about it: You can be sure that a jury would not look favorably on a firm where employees are not alerted to performance issues and are suddenly fired without warning.
- Do not "over-document": You will raise suspicions about your actions if you decide to write up every insignificant thing you can think of because you are determined to force employees out. Lawyers, not to mention judges and juries, are well able to spot over-documentation.
- Do not forget the value of verbal communication: As important as documentation is, it does not require a memo for everything. If a manager has performance issues with employees, the two definitely need to talk about it. Depending on the seriousness of the problem and the extent of their conversation, they may not need to produce a memo. But if the problem continues, make certain to put it in writing. This will clearly show employees what is wrong and it will be on the record that it has been discussed.
- Do not keep secret desk-drawer archives: It is natural for you to want to jot things down that will be helpful to you later, but do not be tempted to keep extensive notes without discussing the issues with employees involved. If employee's performance evaluations and other personnel file documents show no problems but you decide to take adverse action, do not expect to produce your secret notes and make everything okay. Serious employment issues should be discussed and documented in the employee's personnel file. Secret notes look suspicious.
- Do not be stymied by past documentation: It may be that a manager is new to the position or perhaps even inherits a problem employee. If the manager is not satisfied with the job that is being done, but the previous manager never documented any problems, is there a way for them to set things right? Such a situation can be a bit sticky, but it is nothing that cannot be handled. Do not "lower the boom" in a way that would be unfair to someone who is unaware of the problem. It is fair, however, to let employees know "there is a new sheriff in town" and expectations have changed. The documentation can show that the manager talked with employees and determined a timeline

for change. Do not forget to document employee's improvement, too. That can help when performance evaluation time rolls around since it will be easier to justify a raise or promotion that an employee deserves.

- Do not lie or cheat in documentation: In difficult situations, some supervisors might be tempted to make false documentation. Do not do it. First of all, it is dishonest and unethical. If your company or your employee discovers it, a manager could be in big trouble. Second, fake documentation won't help in case of a lawsuit -- in fact, it will cast a large shadow over the manager and will hurt the company's chances of winning the lawsuit. An employee's lawyer will ask detailed questions about the documentation that will uncover the truth – offering anything less increases the risk of being found guilty of perjury.

- Do not manufacture documentation after the fact: Maybe you have employees who have been trouble from the day they were hired. Finally, they get fired. Then you realize you do not have much in the files to justify your action. But you know you had ample opportunities to document many shortcomings. Do not compensate by writing things up and coming up with dates that only *seem* reasonable.

- Do not destroy evidence: Managers have a legal duty to preserve documents that might be relevant to an upcoming legal proceeding. If employees sue the company or file complaints with a government agency or even prepare to file a lawsuit, do not destroy any documentation that relates to employees. Their lawyers will ask the managers under oath whether they willfully destroyed any documentation. Unless they lie about it even then, the deception will be uncovered and could devastate the company's legal case.

Evaluations: A Special Kind of Documentation

Most supervisors would prefer not to fill out performance evaluations. They may plead a lack of time or a lack of anything new to say. They may know that something needs to be said, but they cannot quite put their finger on what it is. Or maybe they hate confronting and criticizing their employees. There is no getting around the fact that evaluations require time and thought if they are going to be worth doing. Keep in mind the goal of performance evaluations is to help employees grow and develop in their jobs. Evaluations provide a mechanism for doing just that. But certain things must be kept in mind:

- Be Honest: You owe it to your employees (and your employer) to be honest. No employee is perfect and no one is perfectly awful. So every evaluation should include both praise and criticism. If you are not telling employees what they need to hear, you are keeping them in the dark about what you need for them to do. You are also keeping your organization from getting the most from its investment in that employee. Perhaps most importantly, remember that dishonest evaluations cause a lot of lawsuits. On the other hand, an honest appraisal gives you and your employees a chance to find out what is at the heart of a problem. Together you can decide on steps that can be taken and timetables to be met to solve the problem.
- Let's Be On Time: Since evaluations can be difficult and time-consuming, they often get set aside. *Do not give in to the tendency to procrastinate*. Besides making employees sweat, a late evaluation sends the signal that managers do not take employee performance seriously. Keep in mind as well that merit raises are often determined by evaluations and it is unacceptable to delay a deserving employee's raise because a manager is too slow in getting the evaluation completed. Since evaluations give managers the opportunity to address problems, highlight accomplishments and focus on goals and employee development, there is every reason to not wait.
- Be Specific: An ambiguous evaluation is not good either. Merely doling out rankings—good, fair, poor—does not tell employees much. The management evaluation forms have space for comments too and managerial comments really provide the meat of the appraisal. Provide examples of good and bad performance. Let employees know what is valued and what must change. If the comment section of evaluation forms is filled with meaningless clichés—"team player," "shows a bad attitude," and the like—not much is being communicated. Give examples to

show how employees are team players. Cite instances showing employee's attitude issues. Do not just write a few vague words and expect to handle the rest during the talk with employees. Remember, if it is not in writing, it is as if it did not happen.

- Set Goals For The Coming Year: Each performance evaluation needs to include specific goals for employees to reach in the coming year. Include the problem areas that were incorporated into the evaluation, such as improving attendance, increasing accuracy, or working faster. Also include things to help employees grow and advance in their career, like taking on additional responsibilities or receiving training.

Enjoy the Payoff of Solid Documentation

As a supervisor, you have developed the skills required for solving workplace problems. You know your employees, their strengths and shortcomings. You know it is important to nip problems in the bud before they blow up in your face. And you know that proper documentation plays a vital role in keeping everything on track. Your use of documentation accomplishes a lot. It shows your employees (and if necessary a judge and jury) that you are treating people fairly and consistently. It warns employees of problems and gives them a chance to fix them. It reduces the likelihood that employees will file suit since disgruntled employees whose files document poor performance or unacceptable behavior won't have strong cases. Most importantly, it bolsters your defense if you do end up in court.

Discipline at Work

Disciplining employees is a crucial part of a supervisor's job. When done properly, discipline can greatly enhance productivity and even improve morale by enforcing the boundaries that an organization has set up for all employees. When employees clearly know what is expected of them, their job is easier and less stressful.

Proper discipline also is important if employees sue for discrimination or illegal firing: The discipline that supervisors impose on employees would be important evidence in court.

However, discipline can be a difficult and unpleasant task, which is why many supervisors fall down on this part of their job. Problems include inconsistent discipline, unfairness, being too lenient or too harsh and not following policies and procedures. By imposing discipline improperly, supervisors can hurt productivity and morale, create the appearance of discrimination or favoritism and create problems in the courtroom in case of a lawsuit.

Fairness

Technically, the law does not require you to be fair when you discipline employees. As long as there is a legitimate motive, it should be technically legal to fire someone even under the most unpleasant circumstances. Terminating older employees who are already facing major challenges in their personal life (e.g., an ailing spouse or health issues of their own) can be construed as heartless, illogical and unfair, so employees may suspect that the manager is hiding something, like discrimination against older people. The risk of older employees suing the company is significant. A jury also would be suspicious of why so "mean" and "unfair" an action was taken and they might believe that the supervisor committed age discrimination, despite all protestations to the contrary.

Consistency

The best way to show the world that you are being fair and honest is to be consistent. Give similar discipline to similar employees who do similar things. Let us say, hypothetically, that an employee, William, has a loud argument with a male co-worker and shoves him in the chest. You decide to fire William because you do not want to tolerate any workplace violence whatsoever. However, when you check with HR, they remind you of Tina, another employee of yours, who last year got into a loud argument with a female co-worker and slapped her hard on the arm. You suspended Tina for a week. A slap could easily be seen as the same as a shove and Tina and William are equally mediocre workers with similar disciplinary records. HR asks you how you will justify the termination in the event that William sues the company for sex discrimination (because Tina received a different form of punishment). You do not have a good answer, so you suspend William for a week, the same as Tina.

Equal treatment of employees does have exceptions. You can treat employees differently based on differences in the people and the situation. If we change the previous scenario to demonstrate that, during William's shove, he was holding a hammer in a threatening manner or that he has had several disciplinary infractions in the past year while Tina has had none in seven years on the job, it is reasonable for you to take different action with William than you do with Tina.

Retaliation Worries
Employees also can claim that your real motive is to punish them for asserting rights protected by law. For example: A manager willfully trumps up employee's attendance problem to punish employees for taking leave under the Family and Medical Leave Act (FMLA) two months ago.

With retaliation and discrimination, the discipline must be fairly severe in order for it to be illegal. A written warning normally would not be serious enough for a court to take action. But if the warning prevents employees from getting a promotion, that could be serious enough to be illegal if your motive for the warning was discrimination or retaliation.

Disciplining Exempt Employees
In general, employees who are exempt from overtime pay under federal law must be paid their full salary for any workweek in which they perform any work. If you have an exempt employee who requires discipline, proceed with caution before docking their pay or suspending them without pay. You can discipline an exempt employee by suspending him without pay only if

- Employees violated a workplace conduct rule (such as your policies on harassment, discrimination, violence, or substance abuse)
- You suspend him for one or more full days
- You impose the punishment in good faith
- You impose the punishment under a written policy that applies uniformly to all workers

In the past, unpaid disciplinary suspensions of exempt employees for violating general workplace conduct rules were allowed only in weeklong increments, but the law was recently changed. In addition, you can dock an exempt employee's pay in any amount for violating a safety rule of major significance.

Legal Issues with Attendance Problems

Several laws give employees the right to take leave. When employees take such leave, it is illegal to punish them for it in any manner, including counting protected absences against them under a "no-fault" attendance policy or points system. Here are several occasions when attendance discipline is a slippery slope:

- FMLA and attendance: In most situations, you must grant FMLA leave even if it causes a hardship on your organization. Your attendance policy must excuse employees' absences protected by the FMLA, including tardiness and partial-day absences. That means you cannot hold FMLA leave against employees in any way, such as poor evaluations or smaller raises. The FMLA entitles certain employees to twelve weeks of unpaid leave when a qualifying event arises, such as the birth or adoption of a child, care of an immediate family member, a serious health condition, or certain exigencies related to the military service of an immediate family member.
- Leave as an ADA accommodation: The Americans with Disabilities Act (ADA) might require you to accommodate a disabled employee's attendance problem with flexible hours or additional time off.

- Religious accommodations: You might have to bend your attendance rules to accommodate employee's religious practice or beliefs under the federal anti-discrimination law known as Title VII or other applicable state law. For example, some religions forbid working on certain days or require people to pray at certain times of the day. In addition employees might need to attend a religious ceremony.
- Military leave: The Uniformed Services Employment and Reemployment Rights Act protects the jobs of employees who miss work for service in the regular military, reserves, or National Guard.

Misconduct Caused By a Disability

Before you discipline employees for misconduct, review the list of laws that might limit your ability to impose discipline, such as the ADA for a disabled employee. Some mental and physical disabilities can cause employees to commit many types of misconduct. As a reasonable accommodation, the ADA might require you to overlook minor misconduct that is caused by a disability, such as a little rudeness. But two aspects of the ADA allow you to hold disabled employees accountable for their conduct:

- Unreasonable accommodations: If allowing the misconduct would be unreasonable; you do not have to accommodate it. Examples include severely rude or unprofessional behavior or refusing to perform an essential duty because of a phobia.
- Direct threat to others: You do not have to tolerate a situation that poses "a direct threat" to other people. In fact, you have a duty to protect co-workers and the public from employees who creates a danger. Example: A mental disability that causes employees to hit a co-worker in anger.

Insubordination That Is Protected By Law

Several types of behavior may seem like insubordination but are actually protected by law.

- Complaining as a concerted activity: The National Labor Relations Act (NLRA) gives all employees, union and nonunion alike, the right to speak out about workplace issues that affect other employees. That is considered to be a "concerted activity," and it is illegal to punish employees for doing it.

- Strikes and walkouts: The NLRA gives all private-sector employees the right to protest by such means as conducting a strike, walkout, or "sickout" or refusing to work overtime. This right belongs to nonunion and unionized employees alike. It even protects one employee who is protesting an issue that affects other employees.
- Unsafe conditions: Under the Occupational Safety and Health Act and the NLRA, employees have the right to refuse to work in conditions that they believe are unsafe. Management is not allowed to discipline them for it.
- Workers' compensation medical restrictions: Workers' comp law may give an injured worker the right to refuse to perform work that would violate a doctor's restrictions.
- Religious refusal to work: If work conflicts with employee religions, you must try to accommodate them. Examples: Employees refuse to work on a holy day; a waitress refuses to sing a birthday song to customers because it would violate her religion.
- Refusing to do an illegal activity: If you tell employees to do something illegal, they may have the legal right to refuse. Certain situations may be protected by a state statute, a whistleblower law or by the broad umbrella of public policy.
- Free speech for public employees: Government employers must be careful not to violate employees' freedom of speech under the US and state constitutions. Public employees' right to criticize their employer must be balanced against the employer's needs, such as preventing disruptions in the workplace.

Disciplinary Systems

There are many systems available for disciplining employees. Many employers use a system called progressive discipline, in which the discipline gets more and more severe if employees fail to correct the problem, progressing from a verbal warning up to termination. In the union context, supervisors have little flexibility and generally must progress through each step before proceeding to the next. This is very limiting. Frequently, the facts and circumstances warrant a different type of discipline. It is better for managers and supervisors to have the flexibility to administer verbal warnings, suspensions, or terminations based upon the seriousness of the particular incident in question, regardless of the employee's prior disciplinary history. For example, the policy might call for managers to typically start with a verbal warning before giving a written warning, but managers have the flexibility to skip the verbal warning based on the situation.

Importance of Progressive Discipline

Progressive discipline provides important negative feedback. Evaluations and discipline give employees an opportunity to correct any problems. Generally speaking, jurors expect this before firing someone. This can reduce the legal risk for your company. When discipline warns employees of problems, they won't be so surprised and angry if they are eventually fired. Therefore, they will have less motivation to seek revenge by suing the company. If they sue the organization anyway, progressive discipline will help convince the court about the legitimate reason for firing employees and that the firm wasn't discriminating illegally.

Typical Steps in Progressive Discipline

There is no perfect progressive discipline system or magic formula for a grievance procedure. Any progressive discipline system provides a framework for letting employees know when there are problems, gives them an opportunity to correct the problems and permits some type of review process before the final decision to fire them is made.

The system outlined below is only an example and it is not necessary for all the items listed to be included in a progressive discipline system. It is also possible for such a system or procedure to have more steps than these:

- *Verbal counseling or warning* -- This is generally the first step. Employees might receive several verbal warnings before progressing to the next step. However, for a serious problem, skip this step. Verbal warnings should always be done calmly, objectively and privately. If managers are angry with employees, they should wait until they can cool down before talking with the employees. It is a good idea to have a second manager present during the verbal counseling as a witness. Managers should document a verbal counseling session by writing a formal memo or informal note and putting it in the personnel file of employees. Despite the apparent contradiction, it is advisable to write down a verbal warning.

- *One or more written warnings* -- This generally follows a verbal warning. As in a verbal counseling session, managers conduct a private meeting with employees. The warning should be written down prior to the meeting (most employers have a form for this). Give employees the warning and let them read it over.   As with verbal counseling, a second manager can be present as a witness. The written warning should have a place for employees to sign, acknowledging that they have received the warning, regardless of whether they agree with the contents of the warning. If employees refuse to sign, another manager or supervisor should be called as a witness to observe that employees have been presented with the warning and refused to sign it and that witness should sign the warning. An adequate written warning should include, at a minimum, the following elements

- The employee's name
- The manager's name
- A specific description of the misconduct or inadequate performance
- The date of the misconduct or poor performance (if appropriate)
- The manager's signature
- The employee's signature
- The signature of a witness (if necessary)
- Add an action plan. With a written warning you may also attach or include a formal "action plan", depending upon the nature and severity of the offense. In addition to the standard elements of

a written warning, a formal action plan may include the following additional elements:

- The steps that employees agrees to follow in order to correct the problem or meet the desired level of performance, attendance, or behavior
- Any commitments of assistance or support that the manager or supervisor has made
- The time frame to be followed in achieving the goal of improved performance, attendance, or behavior
- The consequences that will occur if the performance, attendance, or behavior is not improved within the specified time frame
- If an action plan is created, it will need to be followed up on at the end of the time frame that stated. For example, if employees have thirty days to increase production speed to twenty files per hour, then the manager needs to meet with employees in thirty days to see whether the goal has been met. If the goal has not been met, the manager should administer further discipline. But if the employee does meet the goal, no further discipline should be administered unless the employee suffers a "relapse" in the future.
- *Suspension without pay* -- This may range from one day to two weeks or more, depending upon the circumstances and is almost always unpaid. Some employers will progress immediately from the first suspension to termination for the next offense. If this is your plan, you should state this in the written warning accompanying the suspension. Other employers will try to correct employee's performance or behavior with multiple suspensions of increasing length (e.g., 1-day, 3-day, 5-day, 10-day, etc.). As a general rule, each suspension should be longer than the last, with termination as the final result.
- *Termination* -- Before terminating employees, you should review the personnel file and all relevant documents in order to determine if the termination is appropriate—and defensible in a subsequent lawsuit—given the facts and circumstances. In addition, you should ensure that similarly situated employees have been treated similarly in the past.

Other Forms of Discipline

In addition to the steps outlined above, it is worthwhile to explore other forms of discipline, such as demotion, transfer and reduced raises or bonuses. Many employees can be very satisfactorily managed by economic concerns, such as bonuses and raises.

Other Steps Possible In a Disciplinary System

There are many variations in disciplinary systems, since employers try to create a system that works best for them. Here are some other steps that might be included in a disciplinary system:

- Last-chance agreement: Some employers use a last-chance agreement for employees who could be fired but for whom they want to give one more opportunity to correct their actions. This might be used, for example, with an otherwise great employee found under the influence of alcohol at work twice. The manager may have the employee sign a document that prescribes termination when the situation next occurs. The employee may also be required to submit to frequent drug and alcohol tests (which the company normally does not do).
- Grievance: For unionized employees, a grievance is a formal method for the union to challenge discipline that management imposes.
- A hearing: Some employers give employees a hearing before firing. Most often these hearings will occur in a union setting, where the collective bargaining agreement (CBA) requires a hearing and with government employers, who are required to have a hearing to protect employees' right to due process.

Justifications for Immediate Termination

Some misconduct is so serious that you may want to fire an employee without going through the earlier steps of progressive discipline, such as warnings and a suspension. Despite all earlier warnings to follow the steps of your system, some misconduct is so severe that you simply do not want employees around anymore. Here are some events that might justify immediate firing:

- Stealing or other acts of dishonesty
- Failing a drug test
- Fighting on the job
- Threatening a co-worker or supervisor
- Bringing a weapon to work
- A serious safety violation
- Severe harassment or discrimination

These are just examples. Your company's personnel policies may have a list that is different. For instance, your drug policy might allow employees to fail one or two drug tests before termination. Regardless, there still needs to be consistency, even in the event that you skip progressive discipline steps. Be sure to give similar treatment to similar employees so that your inconsistency might convince the terminated employee think you had an illegal motive.

Disciplining Employees in a Union

If a union represents employees, the company's disciplinary system is most likely governed by the collective bargaining agreement, or CBA. It is important to follow the disciplinary procedures in the CBA. Otherwise, you may find your discipline decisions overturned. The CBA will most likely have progressive discipline steps and allow employees to challenge any disciplinary action through a grievance. Usually, disputes that are not resolved through the grievance process end up in the hands of an arbitrator. In the union context, the decision to discipline or discharge employees will normally be upheld in arbitration if it is based on "just cause". Talk to your HR department if you have any questions about the specifics of your CBA.

Termination

One of the unpleasant realities of managing is that occasionally employees must be separated from the organization because of incompatibility, performance, or any number of other issues. Firing employees is never easy and is one of the most difficult things a supervisor is called upon to do. Even if you do not particularly like the employee; you probably are not looking forward to firing them and the tough conversations that will ensue.

The response you get from firing someone is the most difficult to predict. One employee may thank you for giving them the opportunity to work with you, while another may attempt to engage an immediate supervisor in a fist fight. A job is one of the single most important aspects of our lives. No matter how bad employees are, they no doubt have some measure of pride in their work. Most people spend the majority of their waking hours working and some define themselves by their position. Telling someone "You are fired" can change all of that in one fell swoop.

How you handle a firing will have a tremendous impact on how employees feel about themselves, you and your company. This will, in turn, affect your chance of being sued. In addition, a poorly handled firing will have a negative impact on morale throughout your entire organization. An employment law attorney or human resources consultant can offer suggestions on how to handle the termination and protect a business from the possibility of a wrongful termination lawsuit.

Terminating someone's employment is actually a rather simple action, despite the appearance of having layers of complexity associated with it. In almost every state you can fire employees for almost any reason. There are, of course, exceptions:

- It is illegal to fire someone for a reason that is specifically prohibited by law. For example, you cannot fire employees because of their race or because they take maternity leave.
- Even if your motives are totally legitimate, you do not want to look like you have an illegal motive or else fired employees could sue your company. Then your company might have to pay an employment lawyer tens of thousands of dollars to defend the accusations against you.

The fear of a lawsuit is why most employers are so nervous about terminations. Most organizations have established procedures that must be followed before firing someone. While these procedures may seem like a lot of trouble, keep in mind that they reduce the chance of being dragged into court and accused of discrimination or other wrongdoing.

How to Fire—Step By Step

In this section we will review some preliminary steps you should take before firing anyone. They all are designed to make sure that the termination is motivated by legitimate business reasons. When you have a clear business reason for your actions, fired employees are less likely to think that you are hiding an illegal motive.

More often than not, the most important part of firing employees happens long before you actually tell them that they are fired. If you want to fire someone, it is absolutely essential that you lay the proper groundwork first. That means evaluating employee performance at regular intervals, conducting fair and thorough investigations before firing employees for misconduct, following your company's disciplinary procedures and documenting every decision you make, every step of the way. Let's look at each of these steps:

Give Frequent, Honest Evaluations

Conducting regular performance evaluations offers a multitude of benefits. Apart from the obvious goals of providing employees with guidance and feedback, improving their performance and increasing productivity overall, evaluations can be an effective means of preventing lawsuits. If employees do sue, evaluations can serve as valuable evidence that you fired them for legitimate business reasons rather than because of their race, age, disability and so on.

But evaluations are only as valuable as they are accurate. One of the biggest (and most dangerous) mistakes supervisors make is giving good evaluations to problem employees. From a legal standpoint, the biggest problem is that when you finally reach the point where you can no longer put off firing employees, they have no reason to believe you are firing them because of poor performance. They've always gotten favorable evaluations, so if they were such a poor employee, then you would have told them, right?

The only conclusion these employees can reasonably make is that you had some other, more sinister reason for firing them. Maybe you are being too tough on them because of their gender, race, religion, national origin, age or because they filed a workers' comp claim or because they took time off when a new baby arrived...the list goes on and on. Employees who think they are doing a good job will have an easy time coming up with some illegal reason for why they were fired. Worse yet, why would a jury believe you? If you give employees good evaluations and then fire them for doing bad jobs, you will look like a liar. Your employer might as well attempt to make a settlement in order to make the lawsuit go away as quickly and painlessly as possible.

The solution, of course, is to give accurate evaluations to all employees. Everyone has good points as well as bad, and they all should show up on employee's evaluation. For more advice on how to make evaluations work for you, refer to material previously presented in this book.

It is crucial, as well, for supervisors to give all employees feedback throughout the year. Praise them for doing something well. When they do something poorly, explain what they need to do differently. Frequent feedback will let problem employees know that they are on shaky ground and give them a chance to correct their actions.

Investigate the Facts
Before firing employees for doing something wrong, you must decide whether they actually did what they are accused of. To do that, you have to investigate any allegations, weeding through contradictory statements from different witnesses and deciding who is telling the truth. It is a thankless task, but a necessary one nonetheless. Some investigations are easy: You look at the timesheets and see how many times an employee was late. Some are hard, like an accusation of racial harassment. If the situation is serious enough that you might fire employees, you should get your HR department to help with the investigation.

Use Your Disciplinary System

If your investigation concludes that employees have violated company policy, you need to follow the organization's general disciplinary procedures. For a problem like poor performance, you might start with a verbal warning. If they do not improve, you may progress to a written warning and perhaps an unpaid suspension. These steps will give employees notice that the problem is serious and that they need to improve.

If they do not improve and you eventually fire them, then these disciplinary steps will show that you were fair. If they sue, you will have disciplinary documents to show a jury that you fired them for a legitimate reason.

Watch Out For High-Risk Terminations

Before deciding whether to fire employees, meet with the organization's HR department to evaluate whether there is a high risk of a lawsuit. Some examples where this might be the case include 1) firing the only minority employee in a department; 2) firing a woman who is on maternity leave; 3) firing an older worker whose age you have made fun of. All of these situations look like they might be discrimination or retaliation even if they are not. Or maybe they are. The next section will explore this topic in detail.

High-Risk Terminations

A variety of employment laws make some terminations riskier than others. Discrimination laws, employee benefits laws and unemployment compensation systems can make managers feel like their hands are tied when it comes to firing certain employees.

Do not be too frightened, though. These employees can be fired, but you must do everything correctly so that they do not sue your organization—or win a lawsuit that is unavoidable.

Sometimes it seems that there are certain people you just cannot fire, no matter how incompetent or obnoxious they are. Unfortunately, many supervisors are so afraid of being sued that they are paralyzed into inaction. They keep certain high-risk employees long past the point when they would fire other workers. That can be costly in terms of lost productivity and reduced morale for other employees. It can also be potentially dangerous if, for example, the problem employee shows signs of a violent temper or is harassing other employees.

The employees that you fear the most are likely those who have heightened legal protections, such as federal or state laws which prohibit discrimination or retaliation against them for asserting their legal rights. This applies specifically to employees who really should be fired for legitimate, nondiscriminatory reasons but who often keep their jobs because their employer is too afraid of being sued or other negative consequences. It is valuable to review each of these scenarios in greater detail.

Members of a Protected Class

Federal law prohibits employment discrimination based on certain characteristics called "protected classes." It is illegal to consider these factors for important decisions like termination or demotion:

- *Gender*: Title VII protects both men and women from discrimination on the basis of their gender.
- *Race, color, and national origin:* All employees, including African-Americans, whites and Hispanics, are protected from discrimination on the basis of their race, color, or national origin by Title VII.
- *Religion:* The protections provided by Title VII include all sincerely held beliefs about religion, including religions you may have never heard of, and atheism.
- *Disability:* The Americans with Disabilities Act protects employees with actual or perceived mental and physical disabilities.
- *Age:* The Age Discrimination and Employment Act protects employees forty and older from discrimination on the basis of their age.

- *Pregnancy:* The Pregnancy Discrimination Act includes protections for women who are pregnant or who could become pregnant in Title VII.

In addition, state and local governments may prohibit discrimination on these and other grounds, such as marital status or sexual orientation. As you can see, employees can easily fit into several protected classes. You must completely ignore protected characteristics when deciding whether to fire employees. Make certain that you do not let any hidden biases influence your decision.

Employees on Legally Protected Leave

Any time a manager fires employees who are on or recently returned from some type of protected leave, there is a danger that employees (and the rest of your staff) will think that that is the reason why they were terminated. The suspicion is unavoidable, but there are plenty of techniques to prevent a retaliation lawsuit or, at the very least, justify your decision to a jury.

It is a risky proposition to fire employees while they are on leave from their job. It becomes even riskier when that employee is taking a leave that is protected by a law. Several federal laws require that employers give leave to employees under certain circumstances and also prohibit employers from firing these employees solely because they took leave. The main laws requiring employers to give leave are

- *Family and Medical Leave Act:* The FMLA is almost universally considered to be a complicated and deceptively technical statute that is just waiting to ensnare unwary employers. It pertains to employees' health conditions, family health conditions, childbirth and adoption. (FMLA is discussed in greater detail in an upcoming section).
- *Military leave:* The Uniformed Services Employment and Reemployment Rights Act (USERRA) generally requires employers to grant up to five years of unpaid leave to employees who are members of or join the military. USERRA prohibits

retaliation and discrimination against employees on the basis of their military service.

- *Leave under the ADA:* Disabled employees and job applicants who are qualified to perform the job with or without reasonable accommodation are entitled to the protections of the Americans with Disabilities Act (ADA). They are often referred to as "qualified individuals with a disability." If you have employees who are qualified individuals with disabilities, you must make reasonable accommodations. One form of reasonable accommodation is allowing employees to take leave and returning them to their job once they are able to do so.

More about FMLA

FMLA applies to

- The birth and care of employee's newborn child (applies to fathers, too)
- The care of a child employees adopts or accepts for foster care
- The care employees provides for a child, spouse, or parent with a serious health condition
- An employee's own serious health condition

To be eligible for FMLA leave, employees

- Must have worked for your company for at least twelve months and
- Must have worked for at least 1,250 hours during the twelve-month period immediately before the leave begins.

Employees with an FMLA condition may take up to twelve workweeks of leave during a twelve-month period. For example, employees might take off six weeks when their daughter is born, three weeks to care for their ailing mother and three weeks when they injure their back.

If a husband and wife both work for your company, and they have a baby or adopt a child, they are eligible for twelve weeks combined, not twelve weeks apiece, of FMLA leave.

FMLA leave, by itself, is unpaid. But employees can transform it to paid leave by choosing to use sick leave or vacation days at the same time. In fact, many companies require employees to use their paid leave during FMLA leave.

Sick leave can be used this way only if the FMLA condition is covered under normal sick leave policy. For example, if employees normally aren't allowed to take sick leave when their children are sick, they cannot do so when they take FMLA leave to care for sick children.

Who Is a Child, Parent, or Spouse?
FMLA provides these strict definitions:

- Child: Someone under eighteen who is employee's biological, adopted or foster child, stepchild or legal ward; a child employees is raising as a parent would; an adult child who cannot care for themselves—after surgery, for example.
- Parent: Either employee's biological parent or someone who raised employees as a parent would.
- Spouse: A husband or wife as recognized under state law for purposes of marriage in the state where employees lives. This includes common-law marriage in certain states.

FMLA does not provide leave to care for grandparents, brothers, sisters, in-laws or cousins unless they fall into one of the above categories. Your company probably requires its employees to provide doctor's notes for FMLA leave occasioned by a serious health condition. HR should take care of this. Talk to HR if you think employees are faking or exaggerating their condition. HR has several options, such as getting a second doctor's opinion.

Serious Health Condition
Under FMLA, a serious health condition is an illness, injury, impairment, or physical or mental condition that involves one of the following:

- A condition requiring absence of more than three consecutive calendar days from work, school, or other regular daily activities that also involves continuing treatment by a health care provider. This is the most common situation.

- Pregnancy or prenatal care (including prenatal doctor visits and morning sickness)
- Overnight stay in a hospital
- A chronic condition, such as depression, migraine headaches, asthma, diabetes, epilepsy
- A permanent or long-term condition requiring medical supervision. Examples would be Alzheimer's, stroke, any terminal disease.
- Treatment—such as chemotherapy, physical therapy, dialysis—to prevent a condition from worsening

Except for the first category (more than three days' absence), the condition can last less than three days.

The following conditions normally would not create eligibility for FMLA leave:

- The common cold
- An ordinary case of the flu
- Earaches
- Upset stomach
- Minor ulcers
- Headaches other than migraine
- Routine dental problems
- The taking of nonprescription medications such as aspirin or cold medicine
- An absence, such as a hangover, caused by employee's substance abuse, although treatment for substance abuse is covered.

Intermittent Leave
FMLA for a health condition need not be taken all at once. It can come a little bit at a time. When it does, it is called intermittent leave. Employees may take leave for a short period (a few days or even

a few hours) then return to work until the next time they need intermittent leave. Some examples follow:

- A pregnant woman stays home some mornings because of morning sickness
- Employees with chronic conditions, such as migraines or depression, need to stay home when their conditions flare up
- Employees takes off every Friday to transport a child for kidney dialysis

Intermittent leave can be vexing for these reasons:

- It is often unpredictable. Employees cannot tell you when their next migraine will occur, creating scheduling problems for you
- You might not be able to verify it. You cannot demand a new certification from employees' doctors each time they have a migraine
- It is easy to abuse. An employee who is afflicted with both depression and laziness could "game" the system; you'd be hard-pressed to catch them

It should be said that most employees with chronic FMLA conditions truly are suffering and are being honest with you. But if you think employees are abusing FMLA leave, talk to HR to explore your options.

Exempt Employees and Intermittent Leave

When employees take intermittent FMLA leave for a partial day, you can deduct that time from their pay, even if they are exempt. In this respect, FMLA leave differs from other types of absences. When exempt employees miss work and it is not FMLA leave, you are limited in your ability to dock their pay for it.

Keep Employees' Medical Information Confidential

Recent years have brought increasing emphasis on protecting employees' confidential information, particularly data about their health. Disclosing information about employee's health could run afoul of several laws:

- ADA, which protects the privacy of medical information, even for employees who aren't disabled.
- Privacy laws, which prohibit you from invading employees' privacy.
- The Health Insurance Portability and Accountability Act (HIPAA), which protects the confidentiality of employee medical information gathered through your health insurance plan. Even if HIPAA does not apply to your situation, this relatively new law is making employers very protective of employee health information in general.

Employers should always try to ask employees whether they want their condition disclosed to fellow workers. The manager cannot presume to make that determination for them.

Employees Who Have Contractual Rights

One of the first considerations in firing employees should be whether they have an employment contract. If they do, you must observe the contract terms when terminating employees. This also would include unionized employees where a collective bargaining agreement restricts your ability to fire employees.

Violent or Mentally Unstable Employees

You need to take extra care with employees who show violent tendencies. You do not want them to commit a violent act on the job—or when they are fired. Talk to HR about specific precautions you need to take, but in general be certain that the termination is carried out where others would be in relatively close proximity if you need help and remove all objects from the area that could be picked up and used as a weapon (mugs, staplers, picture frames, etc.).

Employees Who Have Made a Legally Protected Complaint

Traditionally, whistleblowers (employees who report illegal activity) are generally protected from losing their jobs after they blow the whistle. In 2002, a special kind of whistleblower got even more protection. Partly as a result of corporate scandals such as Enron and WorldCom, Congress responded by passing the Sarbanes-Oxley Act. In general, the Act regulates the auditing, financial disclosure, executive compensation and corporate governance practices of publicly traded companies. This law prohibits employers from firing corporate whistleblowers and federal informants.

Retaliation Claims

Many of the same laws that prohibit employment discrimination prohibit retaliation against employees who exercise their rights under those laws. The following federal laws also contain some form of retaliation provision:

- Family and Medical Leave Act
- Fair Labor Standards Act (wage and hour law)
- Occupational Safety and Health Act
- Employee Retirement Income Security Act (benefits)
- National Labor Relations Act (union activity)
- Immigration Reform and Control Act of 1986
- Uniformed Services Employment and Reemployment Rights Act (military leave)
- Employee Polygraph Protection Act
- Sarbanes-Oxley Act (whistleblowers)

What is retaliation? In general, retaliation includes any adverse action taken against employees for filing a complaint or supporting another employee's complaint under one of the above laws. For example, a woman who complains that she was sexually harassed and who was then fired after her complaint is a victim of retaliation.

You cannot retaliate against employees who ask for a reasonable accommodation of their disability under the ADA or who apply for medical leave under the FMLA. It is also illegal to retaliate against employees for opposing an illegal employment practice (even if it does not affect them directly) or for testifying, assisting or participating in any manner in an investigation, proceeding or hearing under one of the above statutes.

Retaliation has become the lawsuit of choice and its popularity is growing. Supervisors need to be especially wary of employees who have filed a previous claim. This does not mean that they are "fire-proof", only that you need to use extra caution.

Preventing Retaliation Claims

Firing employees who have engaged in protected activity is one of the riskiest employment decisions a manager can ever make. Before taking such a step, you need to make absolutely certain that you have observed both the letter and spirit of accepted employment regulations. Not only do you have to make sure employees are not being retaliated against, you also have to do everything you can to avoid the appearance of retaliation.

Perhaps the single most important step to take is to maintain immaculate disciplinary records for all employees at all times—not just after they complain about something. These records will help you prove that you would have fired employees even if they had never engaged in the protected activity. If the employees have several years of subpar evaluations for which they were ultimately fired, you may prevail in a lawsuit even if the timing of the firing is suspicious. Once a complaint has been received, investigate it quickly yet thoroughly, making sure to prevent retaliation against employees along the way.

Making the Decision

Once you make the difficult decision to fire someone, you want to make sure you do it right. When and where should you do it? Who should do the firing? What should you say? What other things should you be concerned about?

How do you decide whether to fire employees? Sometimes the answer is very simple, such as when they are caught stealing. Other times, though, it is not as easy. Maybe the employees have been with you for a long time. You should review every firing decision to double-check that you are making a good decision for a good reason.

Start by taking a look at the goals you want to accomplish by terminating employees. Let us look at some of the common goals to keep in mind during the termination process:

- Keep your eye on the bottom line. The employees may be having productivity problems, may be unable to do the job, or in some other way be affecting your bottom line. Terminating them is probably a wise choice. If you go about firing them in the wrong way, however, your bottom line may suffer more than if you just kept them.
- Work swiftly but carefully. Not all terminations can be carried out with ease, but if you have planned ahead, you can handle a firing without going to Herculean efforts. Nothing is worse than dragging out a termination. Once a decision has been made, work quickly.
- Help employees maintain their dignity. One of your top priorities should be helping employees to maintain their dignity. This is likely one of the most traumatic events in their lives. Treat employees with compassion. You may also be saving your company from a situation where violence may erupt.

Preparing For the Termination Meeting

Firing someone can be traumatic and volatile, so you should plan ahead to make the termination meeting go as smoothly as possible. Here are some important things to do before the termination meeting:

- Try to schedule the meeting for a time when few coworkers will be around, so fired employees can exit without a big audience.
- If you think employees might become violent, talk with HR about security.
- Arrange for someone to delete employees' computer access and security codes while they are in the meeting.
- Arrange for another manager or HR staff to be in the meeting with you.
- Arrange a private place for the termination meeting like your office, the HR department, or a conference room—not in employees' offices (and bring tissues!)

Telling Employees That They are Fired

- Be calm, polite and professional. Be brief and get to the point quickly. Tell employees the truth about why they are being fired or do not say anything at all. Inconsistencies and untruths can undermine legitimate terminations. If employees want to respond, let them. Listen and take notes, but do not argue or apologize. Do not praise employees or try to counsel them—it is too late for that.

- Do not blame "the company" for making you fire them. You *are* the company. Do not say anything that might sound like you have an illegal motive for the termination, like race, color, religion, national origin, gender, pregnancy, or disability. Lastly, do not mention any legal rights employees have exercised, like taking FMLA leave, filing a workers' comp claim, etc. Explain final benefits that employees might receive, like continued health insurance, unused vacation time and final paycheck. Take back company property like keys or a laptop computer. Let employees take their personal belongings from their work area. Ask HR if you need to supervise them.

- Walk them to the front door and wish them well.

Lean On HR

Terminations are difficult and emotional and each one may have unique issues to address. Do not hesitate to lean on HR for advice and support. They have experience, expertise and a unique viewpoint that can help you make the termination process less traumatic.

Workplace Compliance & Violations

> "Each instance of sexual harassment has to be judged on its merits. Facts, timing, motives and creditability: all must be considered before we make up our own minds what to believe." -- Anna Quindlen, New York Times columnist

Sexual Harassment

It should go without saying that sexual harassment in the workplace is wrong. It is also expensive, so all supervisors should be diligent about stopping it. Yet thousands of employers across the country still get slammed by sexual harassment lawsuits each year.

Why does sexual harassment remain such a big problem? Mostly it is because of supervisors, including managers and executives, who just do not get it. They harass their own employees or allow them to be harassed by co-workers and others. Thankfully, they are the minority.

If you are like most supervisors, you are diligent about your job and, as would be expected of a reasonable professional, want to prevent sexual harassment in your company. You would not harass your own employees. You understand blatant sexual harassment and would put a stop to it if you saw it. But you might not recognize some forms of sexual harassment because they are more subtle or may have a twist to them. Further, you might not know exactly what to do when confronted with potential harassment.

The following discussion is designed to help you recognize problems when they occur in your organization. No one expects you to become a legal expert, but you will become familiar with the key concepts, and you will become a better supervisor in the process.

The High Cost of Sexual Harassment

Getting sued for sexual harassment is expensive, win or lose, because

- If employees sues under federal law and wins, your employer might have to pay employees up to $300,000. Most states,

including Pennsylvania, have their own harassment laws where the damages could be much higher.
- Your company has to pay its own attorneys, no matter the outcome. Attorneys' fees can easily extend into six figures.
- Should your company lose the lawsuit it will have to pay the other side's attorneys as well.

Thus, an error in this sensitive area could be a half-million dollar mistake.

Costs Beyond Money
Allowing sexual harassment in your organization can bring damaging publicity to your company. You and your supervisors will find yourselves being grilled on the witness stand. The entire episode can hurt morale and fuel the internal (and external) rumor mill.

It is even worse if you are the perpetrator. Depending on the circumstances, the complaining party could sue you personally. You would be responsible for any damages and attorneys' fees — unless your employer chose to pay them for you. You even could be arrested if assault or sexual battery allegations surface. There is more. You would be disciplined at work. Mild harassment could bring an unpaid suspension, pay cut or demotion (even a written warning would be a dark cloud over your career for years to come). You would likely lose the respect of employees you are supposed to lead, making you less effective as a manager. Lastly, you should bear in mind, that you could be fired as a result of unchecked sexual harassment.

What Exactly Is Sexual Harassment?
We hear about sexual harassment often, but what is it exactly? Legally speaking, sexual harassment is unwelcome conduct based on the victim's gender and it is so severe or frequent that it changes the "terms and conditions of employment" for the victim. Let us break that down:

- Unwelcome conduct: This means that the victim does not like the conduct, whether it is hearing dirty jokes, being patted on the rear end, or seeing a graphic poster on the wall. If the victim welcomes the conduct, it is not sexual harassment under the law, although it might violate company policy. Be careful, though. Some employees might appear unperturbed by questionable conduct even as they do a slow burn on the inside.

- Based on gender: The unwelcome conduct hurts one gender but not the other. For example, a female boss treats men, but not women, like dirt. Or a man gropes a female co-worker but does not touch men. If the conduct is not based on the victim's gender—the boss treats everyone equally badly—it is not illegal sexual harassment, though it could cause other types of legal trouble.
- Severe or frequent: Conduct must be significant to be deemed illegal sexual harassment. It could be one severe incident, such as a sexual assault. Usually, though, it is many smaller incidents—jokes, comments, pictures, touching—that add up to harassment. Either way, it has to be so severe that it changes the victim's working conditions.

A legal term that you may hear is hostile environment, which means pretty much what it says. When sexual harassment makes the workplace extremely unpleasant for employees or employees because of gender, a hostile environment has been created.

Examples of Sexual Harassment

Most sexual harassment lawsuits involve several incidents which, individually, would not be illegal harassment. But when a jury adds them all together, they amount to a verdict for employees. Here are some inappropriate actions that, if unwelcome, could create a hostile environment:

Physical actions

- Groping, touching, or rubbing against someone
- Sexual or crude gestures
- Touching yourself sexually or exposing oneself
- Hugs, kisses, back or neck rubs

Language

- Explicit talk about sex, including jokes and comments
- Comments about someone's body, clothes or looks

- Repeated requests for a date
- Request for sexual favors

Written material
- Sexual graffiti
- Sexual e-mail
- Sexual web sites that others can see
- Sexual magazines or pictures
- Music with explicit lyrics

Keep in mind that these actions must be unwelcome to be illegal harassment. Two friends might enjoy telling dirty jokes, so that technically would not be harassment. (But it could offend the person who overhears it in the next cubicle.)

In some cases, one severe incident can be interpreted as sexual harassment. Examples would be rape, sexual assault, or physical assault.

'Non-Sexual' Sexual Harassment
Strange as it may seem, sexual harassment does not have to be sexual in nature. It can take the form of hostility toward someone because of his or her gender. Most such cases occur when a woman joins a workforce dominated by men—a factory or construction site, for example—and some of the men want to drive her out. Typically, there is a series of hostile actions that can add up to illegal sexual harassment. Some examples follow:

- Violence, including hitting or shoving
- Threats
- Intimidation
- Vandalizing her workstation or personal property
- Sabotaging her work or refusing to help her
- Language that is rude or crude (but not sexual)
- Yelling and arguing
- Cruel practical jokes

In these situations, it may be hard to tell whether the men are motivated by the woman's gender (which could be sexual harassment) or if their actions have nothing to do with her gender (not sexual harassment). If you are not sure, ask HR or your supervisor for help.

Opposite Sex, Same Sex

Statistically, most cases of sexual harassment involve men acting inappropriately toward women. But there are plenty of cases—such as aggressive flirting, sexual language, stalking, and female bosses propositioning male subordinates—of women harassing men.

Same-sex harassment also is against the law. Examples could include a gay supervisor harassing a male subordinate or a lesbian harassing a female co-worker. Harassment of gays and lesbians is a murky area of the law. Federal law does not directly prohibit harassment based on sexual orientation, but lawyers can get around that. In one case, male employees mistreated a gay co-worker who acted overtly feminine. His lawyer convinced a court that this was sexual harassment based on stereotypes of men and women. That is, the co-workers mistreated a man who acted feminine but did not mistreat feminine women.

Also, some states and local governments have laws that specifically forbid harassment based on sexual orientation.

Other Laws to Worry About

When we talk about sexual harassment, we are generally referring to the federal statute known as Title VII of the Civil Rights Act of 1964 or, for example, Pennsylvania's state law equivalent under the Pennsylvania Human Relations Act. In addition, some of the actions we've been discussing can violate other laws. For example, if one employee attacks another because of gender, the victim could sue the employer for sexual harassment, sue the employer and the attacker for assault, sue the employer for failing to prevent the assault and have the attacker arrested for criminal assault.

Harassment is addressed by a multitude of laws that prescribe a variety of potential charges: intentional infliction of emotional distress, false imprisonment, assault, battery, sexual assault, rape, stalking, negligent hiring and negligent supervision. The complete list is actually much longer.

The most important thing you need to know about these laws is this: Any employee who is mistreated in a sexual manner, or mistreated because of gender, can hire a lawyer who will figure out some way to sue your employer for large amounts. So you must stop all inappropriate behavior in your company, regardless of whether or not it fits the legal definition of sexual harassment.

Harassment by Co-Workers
Your company can be liable for sexual harassment by a coworker if it knew about the harassment or should have known because it was so obvious. As a supervisor, you are the company's eyes and ears. If you see harassing behavior or you do not notice it right under your nose, your company "knows" about it and can be held accountable for not stopping it.

Harassers often save their worst behavior until they are alone with their victims, some of whom will endure offensive behavior for a long time before complaining to management. So be on the lookout for inappropriate language or behavior that might be the tip of an iceberg. Consider this scenario:

> You see Jenny openly flirt with a co-worker, Jim, talking in great detail about her sexual exploits from last weekend. Jim, who is married, plays along with her but seems uncomfortable. What should you do? You should immediately stop Jenny's inappropriate language even though it is probably not serious enough, by itself, to be illegal sexual harassment. For all you know, she is doing other things that create a hostile environment for Jim or other co-workers. Tell her immediately (but

privately) that her behavior is inappropriate for the workplace and must stop. Check with HR about following up with Jim and Jenny. You probably should ask Jim if there are other incidents he wants to tell you about and you might want to give Jenny a formal written warning.

Harassment by Others

Your company has a legal duty to provide employees with a workplace free of harassment, no matter the culprit. So you need to prevent and stop inappropriate sexual conduct directed toward your employees by

- Customers, including the big client who thinks an attractive sales rep is included in the purchase price
- Vendors, including everyone from sales to delivery persons
- Independent contractors such as consultants, network administrators, repair personnel, or those brought in to work on a special project
- Temporary employees
- Anyone else who enters your workplace

Courts realize that you do not have much control over some of these people, but you are not helpless. If your employee complains about a crude customer, you could keep employees away from the customer, talk to the customer, or even have your boss contact the customer's boss in some situations.

When Supervisors Harass Employees

Sexual harassment is worse when the harasser is the victim's boss, either a direct supervisor or a higher-level manager. You have power over your employees and power changes everything. Power is the basis for a type of sexual harassment called *quid pro quo*, which is Latin for "this for that." It occurs when a boss offers employees something in return for sexual favors, such as: "Go out with me and you will be promoted." Or it could be a threat: "Sleep with me or you are fired."

Most bosses these days are more subtle in their promises and threats, but this conduct still is sexual harassment. It does not matter if the boss is subtle or vague, or if the promise or threat is unspoken. Supervisors also can commit hostile environment harassment, the same as is committed by co-workers.

Clamping Down on Supervisor Harassment

In 1998, the US Supreme Court decided to get tough on sexual harassment committed by supervisors against subordinates. While the details are lengthy, suffice it to say the court made it much harder for your employer to win a lawsuit if you, as a supervisor, harass a subordinate.

The worst thing you can do is take negative action against employees who refuse your propositions or complain about your inappropriate conduct. This type of retaliation includes firing employees, passing them over for promotion, cutting their hours or pay, or giving them undesirable assignments. Subordinates might be reluctant to complain about your harassment for fear that you will retaliate against them. They might endure the situation for a long time before it becomes unbearable. By the time they complain, you will be facing some serious accusations.

Dating Subordinates

Many employers prohibit supervisors from dating subordinates—and with good reason. It is extremely difficult to fairly supervise someone in this situation. You are not likely to issue a written warning to someone you are dating.

Your other employees will watch the two of you closely, suspicious that you will treat them less favorably than you treat your "sweetheart." If you are male and dating a woman in your department, some co-workers will believe that she does not deserve any rewards she receives — a raise, an important assignment, a cushy trip to a convention — and that she was selected for them just because she is dating you. This may be patently untrue, but the bitterness and rumors will poison your department.

A particularly troublesome feature of romance with a subordinate is when the subordinate feels forced into the relationship, but the supervisor does not realize it. That could be sexual harassment. Many companies have paid dearly when employees claim that their bosses coerced them into unwanted sexual relationships.

Good Love Gone Bad

Perhaps the nastiest aspect of an office romance is the inevitable breakup. Regardless of who initiates the breakup, you will have a hard time ignoring your personal feelings when making business decisions about your former girlfriend/ boyfriend. Sometimes these relationships work out and everyone lives happily ever after. But do not count on it.

Who is a 'Supervisor'?

To understand supervisor harassment, it is useful to know who is considered a supervisor under harassment law. You are an employee's supervisor if at least one of these points applies:

- You have the power to take significant employment actions such as firing, demoting, promoting or giving raises
- You can recommend such actions to the manager who makes the final decision
- You have the authority to direct employee's daily work activities

The "supervisor" category also includes higher-level managers, such as employee's boss' boss.

Finally, harassment law might treat you as employee's supervisor even if you are not. For example, if the chain of command is unclear and the victim of your harassment reasonably believes that you have supervisory power over them, a court might consider you their supervisor.

When Employees Complain of Harassment

Suppose employees approached you right now and said someone was "harassing" them. Would you know what to do? Before that happens—and you never know when it will—plan an appropriate course of action.

As a supervisor, you act on behalf of your employer. If you mishandle the harassment complaint, it is the same as your CEO's mishandling the complaint. If you ignore the complaint, it means your company ignored it. On the other hand, if you handle the complaint properly and treat complaining employees fairly and respectfully, that will go a long way in court if the case ends up there. Perhaps more importantly, treating employees with respect could reduce the chances that they'll sue your company.

Do not take sides, rush to judgment, or make excuses for crude behavior until a full investigation is completed.

Should You Take It to HR?

If employees tell you they were "harassed" or mistreated, listen carefully and thoughtfully. Take notes if necessary. Pay attention to the facts: who, what, when, where. Try to determine if the employees really are complaining about sexual harassment. People sometimes use the term "harassment" for any treatment they regard as unfair. You probably can handle those cases yourself.

Listen carefully to detect evidence of sexual harassment or gender-based misconduct. Even if the employees do not say the words "sexual harassment," it still might be there. The complaint could be sexual harassment if it seems to fit one of these categories:

- The offending language or conduct is sexual in nature, such as sexual comments or touching.
- The accused employee might be treating the complaining employee differently because of gender.
- The complaining employee says it is sexual harassment.

Treat such complaints as possible sexual harassment. Tell the complaining employees that you will take this through proper channels to launch an investigation of the matter. Tell the employees to let you know if the harassment continues or if anyone retaliates against them for complaining.

Next, follow your company's policy on complaints, which probably means going to your human resources department. They have the expertise to conduct a fair and thorough investigation. They'll probably want to separate the employees to prevent further incidents, perhaps suspending any accused employee with pay.

Prevent Retaliation

Once employees complain about harassment, you must be sure that no one retaliates against them. Retaliation means harassing or discriminating against them to punish them for complaining. Should that happen, they could sue your company for harassment and retaliation. Examples of retaliation follow:

- Termination
- Demotion or undesirable assignments
- Reduced pay
- Denial of a raise
- Bad treatment from co-workers, including sabotaging her work

Being sued for retaliation is actually more dangerous than a harassment complaint. Jurors tend to come down hard on employers who retaliate or allow employees to retaliate. Worst of all, your company might have to pay for a retaliation verdict even if there was no illegal harassment. The law protects employees' right to complain, even if their complaints are off the mark.

After the Investigation

There are several possible results of an investigation into a complaint:

- Inappropriate conduct occurred: Offending employees should be disciplined for their conduct and warned not to do it again.
- You cannot tell if inappropriate conduct occurred: Investigations often are inconclusive. The complaint might pit one person's word against another while the truth remains elusive. Maybe something happened, but HR cannot decide exactly what it was. You and HR should talk to one or both of employees about ways to avoid such conflicts or misunderstandings in the

future. But no one is disciplined and you do not hold the matter against either employee down the road.

- Inappropriate conduct did not occur: Perhaps it was all a misunderstanding, or perhaps the accused employee said something that was crude but not serious enough to violate company policy.

- The complaining employee lied: Sometimes employees fabricate an accusation of sexual harassment. Tread cautiously here. Law textbooks are replete with cases of bosses who got their employer sued by incorrectly accusing a harassment victim of lying. If you think a complaint is false, let HR deal with it.

What Type of Discipline?

Some bosses think that inappropriate sexual conduct should mean automatic dismissal. A better approach might be to let the punishment fit the crime. Some violations deserve termination, but depending on the facts of the case, other types of discipline might be more appropriate. Such disciplinary actions could include unpaid suspension, demotion, written warning, or a verbal warning. Be sure that any discipline is documented in the offending employee's personnel file—even a verbal warning—in case of more trouble in the future.

Discrimination and Other Forms of Harassment

When people hear the word "harassment," many think of sexual harassment. While sexual harassment gets most of the headlines, discrimination and harassment complaints based on other protected classes remain major problems for employers. As with most employment matters, supervisors are key players in preventing discrimination claims. Discrimination can be committed only by an employer or an employer's representative--namely, you. Because they make so many decisions about employees, supervisors often are the parties accused of discrimination. If you carelessly ignore discrimination laws, you can provoke employees into filing costly public lawsuits against your company.

On the other hand, if you carefully avoid committing discrimination—or even the appearance of discrimination—you will have a happier, more productive staff that is less likely to sue. Your quiet good work may not generate media headlines, but you can take comfort in a job well done—and your superiors will appreciate your value to the company.

What constitutes discrimination and how can you avoid it? Let's take a look.

Discrimination in the 'Good Old Days'

Back in the 1950s, supervisors did not worry about discrimination because it was legal. White men had the best jobs and highest pay. Women generally were expected to stay home and raise the kids, or they could do "women's work" and become teachers, secretaries, or nurses. In fact, at one time female teachers could not be married—they had to quit their job upon marriage. Men often would be paid more than women doing the exact same work because men were supposed to "bring home the bacon." Employees often were forced to retire at age 65 whether they wanted to or not.

Today, such blatant discrimination seems foreign to us, since it was outlawed by Title VII of the Civil Rights Act of 1964, known more simply as Title VII. That is the primary federal law that prohibits employment discrimination based on the protected classes of race, color, gender, religion, and national origin. States such as Pennsylvania followed suit, passing their own anti-discrimination statutes. Federal laws were later expanded to include disability and family medical leave protection. It would be naïve to believe that discrimination has vanished, but it is not as blatant as it once was.

Discrimination against Protected Classes

Illegal discrimination occurs when employers take significant adverse actions against employees or job applicants because of their protected class. You are probably familiar with many of these protected classes, but some on the list below may surprise you:

- Race
- Color
- Gender/sex (including pregnancy and equal pay)
- National origin
- Citizenship
- Age
- Military service
- Union activity
- Disability
- Religion
- Family Medical Leave

Illegal discrimination boils down to your motive for taking action against employees. For example, it is perfectly legal to fire 50-year-old sales reps for missing their quarterly sales goal. But if you do not fire 25-year-old reps that also miss their sales goals, you are giving at least the appearance of age discrimination unless you have a legitimate reason for treating the second group differently.

Race
Title VII protects all races, including African-Americans, Caucasians, and Hispanics. The victim can be the same race as the perpetrator or a different race. For example, you might have a Hispanic supervisor discriminating against a white employee; a Native American discriminating against a Hispanic employee; or an African-American discriminating against a white employee.

Color
Under Title VII, color almost always means the same as race. An exception could be a light-skinned African-American supervisor discriminating against a dark-skinned African-American.

Gender/Sex
Title VII protects both sexes. The perpetrator could be motivated by either a dislike for, or an attraction to, one gender. For instance, a female supervisor thinks women are easier to work with, so she discriminates against a male applicant by hiring a less-qualified woman.

Equal Pay Act

A type of sex discrimination with deep historical roots is paying a woman less than a man for the same work. The EPA requires equal pay for men and women who perform equivalent work. If a man and a woman in your department are getting significantly different pay for the same work, you must have a legitimate reason for the disparity, such as a difference in experience, education, skill, or productivity.

Pregnancy

The Pregnancy Discrimination Act prohibits discrimination against women because they are pregnant or may become pregnant.

National Origin

Title VII defines national origin as the country where you were born or where your ancestors came from. National-origin lawsuits often overlap with religion (a Muslim from Iraq) or race (a Hispanic from Spain). Discrimination and harassment based on national origin also are prohibited by the Immigration Reform and Control Act (IRCA), which applies to employers with as few as four employees.

Citizenship

IRCA also prohibits employers with at least four employees from discriminating based on citizenship. That is, you cannot reject a job applicant only because they are not a US citizen--provided they are authorized to work in this country. You also cannot treat employees differently on the basis of their citizenship or give advantages to US citizens.

Age

The Age Discrimination in Employment Act (ADEA) protects people forty and older, so you cannot consider their age when making employment decisions. A typical lawsuit involves a supervisor who may have made disparaging comments about older employees' ages—"they are older than dirt", "old people are too slow", "it is time for them to retire to a nursing home." While this behavior may be considered rude and boorish, it is not actionable yet. When the supervisor fires or lays off the older employees, they figure that it must be because of their age. If the employees sue, the supervisor's prior comments will make it hard and expensive for the employer to win the lawsuit.

Military Service

The Federal Uniformed Services Employment and Reemployment Rights Act prohibits discrimination against employees who take leave for service in the military or National Guard. Talk to HR if you have employees whose military service is interfering with work.

Union Activity

The National Labor Relations Act prohibits discrimination or retaliation against employees because of their union activity or other concerted activity. This situation usually arises at a nonunion company where management does not want a union presence. You cannot fire someone only because they are trying to unionize your employees. Neither can you refuse to hire candidates because they were union leaders at their previous job.

Union law is quite complex and a lot of it does not make sense to the casual observer. If you are confronted with a union issue, go straight to HR or Legal for advice.

Disability

The Americans with Disabilities Act (ADA) protects people with mental or physical disabilities. As with other discrimination laws, you cannot take adverse action against others because of their disabilities, such as refusing to hire candidates just because they have cancer or a serious mental condition.

Accommodations

The ADA requires employers to go further than other discrimination laws. You must offer help — a reasonable accommodation — to disabled employees who need assistance doing the essential duties of their job. Depending on the medical condition, an accommodation could be almost anything, including

- Eliminating a nonessential duty
- Buying equipment to help employees
- Making a minor modification to your building
- Assigning a co-worker to provide reasonable help as needed
- Allowing more breaks or days off
- Allowing a different work schedule, flex time or telecommuting
- Authorizing a reasonable leave of absence

Employers do not have to make accommodations that are unreasonable or create an undue hardship, but even reasonable accommodations could carry significant cost or create some difficulties for you.

Before deciding whether to provide employees with accommodations, you must determine whether they qualify as a disabled person under the ADA. This can be a difficult determination. If you have employees or job applicants who you think might be disabled, go directly to your HR department. If HR decides that a disability exists, you must consider providing reasonable accommodation. If a disability does not exist, do not proceed as if one does. That could create major legal complications downstream.

So what constitutes a disability? Although you may not be making disability determinations, you still should know what a disability is under ADA. That way, you will know when to go to HR for help. An ADA disability is any physical or mental condition serious enough to substantially limit major life activity such as seeing, hearing, talking, or walking. The rules tend to be less than clear-cut, leaving determinations to be made on a case-by-case basis. Here are some examples:

- AIDS—Yes consider it a disability
- Permanently uses a wheelchair—Yes
- Lifting restrictions—Generally no
- Cancer—Yes in many cases
- Blindness—Total blindness is a disability, but poor vision usually is not
- Drug addiction—Past drug addiction can be a disability; recent or current drug use is not

- Alcoholism—Yes, an alcoholic in recovery can be protected
- Depression—Very serious cases, yes. Mild cases, no
- Obesity—Morbid obesity (double normal weight) can be
- A typical broken leg—No
- Stress—Not by itself, but it could be part of a mental disability
- Carpal tunnel syndrome—No in most cases, maybe in severe cases
- Diabetes—Serious cases could be

An employer may require that disabled employees not pose a "direct threat" to the health or safety of themselves or others. Examples: A mental illness makes someone too violent to work around others; employees with a muscle disease are too weak to drive a forklift safely.

If the direct threat is the result of a disability, the employer must determine whether a reasonable accommodation will either eliminate the risk or reduce it to an acceptable level. If no such accommodation is possible, the employer may refuse to hire an applicant or discharge employees who pose a direct threat.

Past Disability
ADA protects employees who were disabled in the past, such as a cancer patient who has been cured or is in remission. Consider this scenario:

You need to promote someone and the best-qualified person is Julia. You know that she once was committed to a mental institution, but doctors controlled her condition eight years ago, so she is not disabled now. You worry, though, that elevating her to a stressful position could cause a relapse. Even though you have no evidence to support your speculation, you award the promotion to someone less qualified. You just committed disability discrimination against Julia.

Regarded As Disabled
Under ADA, the third definition of disability covers those who have been "regarded as having such impairment." This definition is intended to

protect employees with a physical or mental impairment that does not substantially limit a major life activity, but who is treated by an employer as having a limiting disability. This definition also applies to an individual who has a physical or mental impairment that substantially limits a major life activity only as a result of the attitudes of others about the impairment. Here's an example:

> If employees have controlled high blood pressure that is not a disability, their supervisor cannot reassign them to less strenuous work because of unsubstantiated fears that they'll suffer a heart attack if they continue to perform strenuous work. Although the employees are not disabled, the supervisor "regards" them as disabled, so the ADA protects them from discrimination.

Qualified for the Job

For disabled employees to be covered by ADA, they must be "qualified" for the position in question. This means they can perform the "essential functions" of the position—with the help of a reasonable accommodation, if necessary. Essential functions might include

- Using a computer
- Interacting with customers
- Standing (if the job cannot be done sitting down)
- Moving 50-pound objects (by lifting or other means)

Religion

Title VII protects sincerely held religious beliefs and the practices required by these beliefs. This could include beliefs that aren't part of an organized religion yet occupy a place in believers' lives similar to that filled by the idea of God. Atheists and agnostics are protected. However, courts have ruled that being a Skinhead or following the philosophy of the Ku Klux Klan would not constitute religious beliefs under Title VII.

As with other protected classes, you cannot take adverse action against employees because of their religion (or lack thereof). The following actions could be illegal religious discrimination:

- Trying to convert employees to your religion and firing them when they refuse
- Suspending a Jewish employee for misconduct but not disciplining a Christian for the same type of misconduct
- Refusing to hire Muslims

In these examples, you can substitute any religion. They all apply.

Exceptions for Religious Organizations

The law is a bit different for churches and religious organizations, which can require employees to hold certain religious beliefs for jobs related to the religious mission of the organizations. The Roman Catholic Church, to cite one instance, is permitted to hire only Catholics to be priests, but it cannot require its maids to be Catholic.

This exception applies only to organizations whose purpose is religious in nature. It would not apply, for example, to a computer consulting firm whose owner is devout. The owner cannot hire employees based on their religion because the company's primary mission is repairing networks and not souls.

Accommodating Religious Practices

When employees' religions interfere with work, Title VII requires that the employer try to make a reasonable accommodation for the employees' religion. But you do not have to make an accommodation that would be an undue hardship on your business. The obligation to accommodate employees' religious beliefs is not as strict as the duty to accommodate disabled employees under ADA.

So if employees request time off to observe a religious holiday, you must allow them to do so unless it would create an undue hardship for your company. Undue hardship basically means a significant disruption or expense. But do not refuse requests for accommodation before you talk to HR.

Adverse Actions

The following actions normally are serious enough to be illegal discrimination if they are motivated by protected class membership. All of these actions, however, are legal if based on legitimate business reasons:

- Termination or selection for layoff
- Pay cut
- Reduction in hours or denying the opportunity to earn overtime
- Demotion
- Failure to hire
- Failure to promote

Note that all these actions hit employees in their pocketbooks. Courts are most concerned with discriminatory actions that hurt employees' abilities to earn a living or advance in their career.

Lesser Actions

Many other actions you might take against employees do not rise to the level of discrimination by themselves, but they can lead to more serious action down the road that is discrimination. For example, giving a written warning is not serious enough to be discrimination until it later causes employees to be laid off, passed over for promotion, or given a smaller raise than they would have received without the warning on their record. Some other examples include

- Giving a poor evaluation to employees because of their race;
- Denying a lucrative assignment to pregnant employees because you assume they would not want all the travel involved.

Subtle Forms of Discrimination Today

It is rare today to hear supervisors openly admit they won't hire a minority. Instead, they'll be more subtle, finding a weakness with every minority applicant. Then they'll declare that the best candidates happen to be white. Sooner or later someone—maybe a highly qualified minority candidate, maybe another manager who notices that the department has no racial diversity—will get suspicious. Then those supervisors could be in big trouble.

Subconscious Discrimination

Some people discriminate without really thinking about it. For example, a female supervisor might give a stern written warning to a man who is tardy too many times and ends up getting fired. But the supervisor may have sympathy for a woman with children who does the same thing and does not write her up at all.

A large number of people have absorbed some stereotypes on the subconscious level. Even open-minded, educated supervisors who would never consciously want to discriminate against anyone can be vulnerable to this. An interesting resource for evaluating personal subconscious stereotypes is called Project Implicit® from Harvard University. On their website (https://implicit.harvard.edu/implicit/research), several free and anonymous tests are provided for individuals to test their subconscious or implicit biases in a variety of ways.

Ignorant Discrimination

This refers to supervisors who discriminate intentionally because they do not know enough about the law. They may realize that gender discrimination is illegal, but other situations are beyond them.

For example, a National Guard reservist says he needs a month off because he volunteered for special training on the other side of the country. The boss, uninformed though he or she may be, says "Sorry, but we cannot keep your job open that long." That is discrimination.

Disparate Impact Discrimination

"Disparate impact" is what lawyers say when you make a decision based on legitimate reasons, but the impact is harsher on employees in one protected class, such as women. Disparate impact discrimination is uncommon, but it does happen. Consider this case:

A warehouse manager decides that everyone in the position of Dock Assistant I must be able to lift 100 pounds, which lets them do any job in the warehouse. This sounds legitimate, but it forces almost all female employees into the lower-paying position of Dock Assistant II. Lifting 100 pounds may not really be essential because the warehouse has forklifts, dollies, and carts to help with heavy loads. This policy could be sex discrimination.

Customer Preferences

Sometimes a customer asks you to commit illegal discrimination. For example, a major customer might request a sales rep who is a pretty young woman. If you accede to the request, you could be committing sex discrimination against your male reps or age discrimination against your male sales reps over 40.

Check Your Motives

The next time you are pondering adverse action against employees, such as termination, suspension, demotion or denial of promotion, do a reality check on your motives. Did employee's race, age or other protected class have any effect on your decision? Would you make the same decision if employees were a different religion or gender? If you have any bias against a particular protected class, make sure it does not influence your actions.

Retaliation – The Hidden Danger

If an employee accuses you or your employer of discrimination, be careful not to retaliate. As previously discussed, retaliation is illegal and can be just as expensive a judgment as discrimination.

Retaliation can take many forms, such as inventing a reason to fire a woman after she accuses you of sex discrimination, or cutting the hours of a Christian employee who complained about religious discrimination.

After employees makes a complaint, check with HR or a labor law specialist before taking any adverse action, even if you think it is deserved.

Document, Document, Document

The best way to avoid being accused of discrimination is to keep meticulous written records of all important events and decisions. This includes accurate evaluations for all employees and written warnings that go in their personnel files. If you are ever accused of discrimination, your documentation will be written evidence that you had good business reasons for your actions.

Understanding Wage & Hour Law

The proper payment of wages seems as though it should be a straightforward matter. Employees work their hours, the company pays their wages and that should be that. Unfortunately, wage and hour law is more complex than that. Under the Fair Labor Standards Act (FLSA), companies must be concerned about a number of sometimes thorny questions, including proper remuneration for employees who

- Work off the clock
- Take work home
- Work through lunch or breaks
- Put on equipment before clocking in
- Request or receive comp time
- Travel on company business

If you manage exempt employees, other, equally complex issues might arise. As a supervisor, you must do your part to make sure your employees are paid all the money they've earned—not too much or too little.

In some situations, however, the law makes it difficult to determine how many hours employees must be paid for. If you underpay employees, they could complain to the state or federal department of labor, or they could sue your company. Many businesses have been hit with class-action lawsuits, where hundreds or thousands of employees sue their employer and claim millions of dollars in unpaid wages.

In this section, we'll explore issues that are vital for every supervisor to know. This information will help you avoid obvious problems—an hourly employee working during lunch, for instance—and to recognize red flags so you can alert your company's HR or payroll departments.

Exempt and Nonexempt Employees
FLSA distinguishes between exempt and nonexempt employees and treats them very differently.

Nonexempt employees : Chances are that most or all your employees are nonexempt and must be paid time-and-a-half when they go beyond 40 hours in a workweek. They usually are paid by the hour.

Exempt employees: Most often, they are paid a weekly salary which typically stays the same no matter how many or how few hours they work that week. Exempt employees most commonly are in management, high-level jobs, or specialties.

We'll discuss exempt and nonexempt employees in more detail later.

Minimum Wage
You must pay the minimum wage to all employees—exempt and nonexempt alike. A number of states' minimum wage laws have surpassed the federal standards and require non-exempt employees to be compensated at higher levels than federal mandates. Potential problems can arise regarding employees whose pay varies because they are paid by commission or by piece rate. Trouble also can occur when employees with a low weekly salary works very long hours.

Discrimination
Under various discrimination laws, employee pay cannot be based on race, color, sex, pregnancy, religion, national origin, citizenship, disability or age. This prevents a biased supervisor from paying less to minorities, for example. In addition, the Equal Pay Act (EPA) requires equal pay for men and women who perform equal work. This gives employees more protection than other discrimination laws because you could violate the EPA even without intending to discriminate. If employees file an EPA lawsuit, the court will look at your shop and compare the pay of men and women doing similar work. If one gender makes significantly more and

you do not have a good business reason for it, your company will likely lose the lawsuit. EPA does not apply to race or other protected characteristics.

Retaliation

It is illegal to punish employees for complaining to a court or government agency that your company violated FLSA. In most cases, the law also protects employees who complain to management about pay.

State and Federal Laws

Each state has its own set of wage and hour laws. In Pennsylvania, for example, employees can file complaints with the Department of Labor and Industry's Wage and Hour Division or to its federal counterpart, the US Department of Labor. State and federal agencies can prosecute offending employers and employees can privately sue employers under state and federal laws.

Paycheck deductions: Some states prohibit you from deducting money from paychecks without employee permission or court order.

Minimum wage: Some states and cities require a minimum wage higher than the national figure.

Terminated employees: A number of states impose deadlines for providing employees their final paychecks after they quit or are fired. Examples of covered issues include

- Commissions owed to employees
- Any debts employees owe you
- Payment for unused vacation time
- Leave time that was used but not yet earned

Managing Nonexempt Employees

FLSA requires that nonexempt employees be paid overtime when they work more than forty hours in a workweek. They must be paid at least "time and a half"—one -and-a-half times the regular rate of pay for hours over forty in a workweek, even if they are salaried.

Pay Nonexempt Employees for All Hours Worked

Among the key issues associated with overtime is how to calculate the number of hours employees have worked in a given workweek. In other words, what activities qualify as work time?

In general, you must pay employees for all time they work, whether on company premises or at any other prescribed place of work. The US Department of Labor usually will assume that employees worked from the time they clocked in until they clocked out. So if the workday is 8:00 a.m. to 5:00 p.m. and some nonexempt employees regularly clock in, say, five minutes early or clocks out five minutes late, you probably will have to pay them overtime for the extra time that accumulates.

Watch the Clock

As a supervisor, you are responsible for properly counting your employees' hours. It is not always as easy as it seems. Time clocks and time sheets work well for keeping track of employee hours, but they are not perfect. If your time clock malfunctions, you must pay nonexempt employees for all the time they actually work. Should employees forget to clock in, you still must pay them for all the hours they work.

You can discipline employees for time clock violations — after all, following your company's time clock rules is part of their job. Save this for serious violations, such as repeatedly forgetting to clock in or out, or clocking in a co-worker who hasn't arrived at work yet.

Donning and Doffing

"Donning and doffing" is the legal term for putting on clothes and equipment and taking them off again. It has become a hot topic in court. Employees are demanding to be paid for the time they spend preparing to work, such as putting on uniforms and safety equipment. For example, employees might spend ten minutes putting on safety equipment before clocking in, then ten minutes taking it off at the end of the day after clocking out. That is twenty minutes per day, five days per week, 52 weeks a year, multiplied by the number of your nonexempt employees. Clearly, a lot of money is at stake in the donning and doffing discussion. It is not necessary to understand all the details of this complex area of law, but you should be prepared to contact HR if you see a questionable situation.

Break Time

The US Department of Labor generally does not require you to give employees breaks, although many states do. You must pay nonexempt employees for breaks of less than thirty minutes, which means you cannot subtract breaks, meals, smoking breaks, telephone breaks, and so on from the number of hours worked unless they are at least thirty minutes long.

State law may have special break requirements for employees who are minors. For example, Pennsylvania requires employers to give minors a break of at least 30 minutes if they are otherwise working more than five continuous hours without a break or rest period.

Although federal law does not generally require employers to provide breaks to their employees, one exception is for employees who are nursing mothers. The FLSA was amended in 2010 to require employers to allow lactation breaks for up to one year after the birth of a child. There is no limit to the number or duration of these breaks except that they must be reasonable, and the employer must provide a private area for nursing other than a bathroom.

Employees must be completely relieved of their duties during unpaid breaks. If they are not, such breaks must be included in hours worked. That means you must pay them overtime if adding their break time to their hours worked results in more than forty hours in a given week. Employees are not considered completely relieved of their duties if

- They face frequent interruptions during breaks
- They are required to attend meetings or be "on call" to return to work at a moment's notice
- You place restrictions on what they can do or where they can be during their breaks

Let us say your nonexempt repair specialist eats his lunch in fifteen minutes. Then the copier breaks and you ask him to fix it, which takes five minutes. You tell him to take the remaining fifteen minutes of his lunch. In this situation, you must pay him for his lunch break since he wasn't off for thirty consecutive minutes.

You also must pay nonexempt employees for any time during which they are "suffered or permitted to work." That means you have to pay overtime to employees who rack up extra hours by voluntarily working through lunch—even if you've specifically told them not to.

On-Call Time

What if you allow a nonexempt employee to go home but require them to answer work-related phone calls or be on call to work on short notice? What pay are they entitled to? It depends on how much freedom they have.

Waiting to Work: If they are pretty much free for personal activities and the phone calls from work are infrequent, you probably do not have to pay them for the on-call time when they are not actually working.

Waiting IS Their Work: If being on call greatly restricts their personal life, you probably must pay them for the entire time they are on call, including the time when they are merely waiting to be called. If they get frequent phone calls from the shop or must stay near their work site the entire time, you will probably have to pay them for all this time.

Unauthorized Work

Common sense tells us that we do not have to pay overtime to employees who work extra hours after being told not to. But overtime is an area of the law where common sense can get you into trouble. The truth is that even if you have a rule prohibiting employees from putting in overtime hours without prior authorization, you still have to pay them overtime if they work more than forty hours in a week. The burden is on you to ensure that they do not do so.

Imagine that you have a gung-ho, eager-to-please employee. You know that he brings work home at night and on weekends without asking for overtime pay. It seems harmless until he demands his OT for every week over the past two years. Should he sue for that money, a court likely would order your company to pay him for, say, 1,000 hours at time-and-a-half, plus additional damages.

The point here cannot be emphasized enough: Once extra hours are worked, the extra compensation must be paid.

That does not mean your only choice is to sit back and hope employees follow the rules. Your best approach here is to make sure that employees do not in fact work more than forty hours a week. Enforce your company's overtime policies consistently. If employees work extra hours without authorization, let them know in no uncertain terms—preferably in writing—that they cannot work overtime without your authorization and that they will be disciplined if they continue to do so.

If employees put in more overtime hours after receiving this type of warning, you should follow your disciplinary procedures the same as you would for other violations of company policies, up to and including dismissal. At no point, however, are you relieved of the obligation to pay employees for all hours worked. Here are some tips to prevent unauthorized work:

- Keep an eye on employees to make sure they aren't working before hours, after hours or through lunch
- Consider prohibiting employees from taking breaks at their desks or workstations
- Periodically patrol the work area during lunch to enforce the rule against working during lunch breaks
- Require employees to get permission before working at home

Travel Time
Deciding when to pay nonexempt employees for travel time can be challenging. Normally, you do not have to pay employees for traveling to and from home.

Travel during the workday
If employees must report to one work site, then travel to another site, their travel time to the second site is on the clock.

Out-of-town travel: You must pay employees for any time they spend traveling outside of their home communities for work-related purposes. This is true even if the travel occurs on their normal day off, such as Saturday.

These constitute the legal requirements; your company might choose to be more generous.

Do not give Comp Time Instead of Overtime
Some bosses violate FLSA by giving nonexempt employees time off-- called compensatory time or comp time—instead of overtime pay. For example, if employees work an hour of overtime this week, you cannot let them go home early one day next week. Unless you work for the government, comp time is flat-out illegal.

Employees might ask you for comp time—even beg you for comp time— but it is still illegal. Those employees would still have the right to sue your company for giving them comp time instead of OT pay.

In the private sector (meaning you do not work for the government), the only other option is to "flex" a nonexempt employee's work hours within the same workweek. For example, if they work an hour late on Thursday, you tell them to leave an hour early on Friday to keep them at forty hours for the week. Since it is all in the same workweek, you do not owe any overtime pay. This is legal only if it all occurs in the same workweek.

Comp Time for Exempt Employees
Exempt employees are not entitled to OT pay, so giving them comp time is generally OK under FLSA.

Comp Time for Government Employees
If you are a public employer, you can give employees ninety minutes of comp time for every hour of overtime worked. But you cannot let

employees accumulate more than 240 hours of unused comp time. For public employees in public safety or seasonal jobs, the limit is 480 hours.

If you are a public-sector employer that gives comp time, your policy should limit the amount of comp time employees can accumulate. In other words, you can force them to use their comp time.

Managing Exempt Employees

With exempt employees, your two main concerns are

- That they really are exempt under the FLSA
- That you do not do anything that would ruin their exempt status

Misclassifying Employees as Exempt

Since exempt employees are not eligible for overtime, it is tempting to classify as exempt as many employees as you can. This is a fertile area for mistakes. Most exempt employees are what are called "white-collar exemptions." This category includes administrative, executive, and professional employees; computer professionals; and outside sales employees. Many managers and supervisors fall into this category as well. The main requirements for employees to be exempt under the white-collar rules are

- *Employees must perform exempt tasks:* The primary work must consist of higher-level duties, such as professional, executive, and administrative responsibilities. If a manager spends more than 50 percent of his time on non-management duties, he's probably not exempt.
- *Employees must be paid a minimum amount:* Most white-collar exemptions require employees to be paid a minimum salary of $455 per week--$23,660 annually.
- *Employees must be paid on a "salary basis":* You must treat white-collar employees a certain way to avoid paying them overtime. For example, you cannot dock their salary for most partial-day absences. (More on that below.)

Forty-Hour Workweeks

Employees sometimes think their exempt status allows them to work whenever they want without any consequences because no one is keeping track of their hours. They might make a habit of showing up late and leaving early even though they are clearly expected to work forty hours a week.

In fact, you can require exempt employees to work forty hours a week—or even fifty or sixty. If someone works less than 40 hours, you can make them use vacation time for the shortage. You also can discipline them for this attendance violation.

Docking the Pay of Exempt Employees

In general, exempt employees must be paid their full salary every week they work, regardless of how much or how little they work. But there are limited opportunities to dock the pay of an exempt employee who misses work:

- *Health-related absences:* When exempt employees run out of sick days and miss at least one day of work, you can dock their pay in one-day chunks. But you cannot deduct any pay for a partial-day absence. Example: Employees who miss two-and-a-half days can have two days of pay deducted.
- *FMLA leave:* If an absence is covered by FMLA, you can deduct it from employee's pay—even for partial days. Example: Pregnant exempt employees who take three hours of FMLA leave to see their doctor can have their pay reduced for the time lost. They could elect to use sick leave instead.
- *Personal leave:* When exempt employees are absent for personal reasons (not sickness or disability), you can dock their pay in one-day chunks. But you cannot dock their salary for partial day absences. You may require them to use vacation time for full-day or partial-day absences.
- *Safety violations:* If exempt employees violate major safety rules, you can discipline them by docking their pay in any amount.

Other Exemptions

Beyond white-collar exemptions, FLSA includes a hodgepodge of other exempt jobs. Among them are sales reps, farm workers, and certain local delivery drivers. The list also includes some unusual occupations, such as employees who process maple sap into syrup and those who work at home fashioning wreaths from evergreen branches.

For positions on this long and sometimes bewildering list, you generally do not have to pay time-and-a-half for OT. Check with HR or Payroll for a more comprehensive look at the exemptions list.

Safety and Workers Compensation

According to the National Institute for Occupational Safety and Health, on average, sixteen American workers die every day as a result of workplace mishaps. In addition, roughly four million workers are seriously injured each year. That equates to nearly 11,000 reported workplace injuries every day of the year.

Managers can play a major role in preventing such injuries. Unlike senior executive, managers and supervisors see their employees and their workplaces daily. They are the eyes and ears of the company and they set the tone for their employees. If supervisors send the message that safety is important, employees will reflect it.

Workers' compensation laws provide protection to employees in the event that they are injured in the performance of their job. In such cases employees are able to receive compensation for any temporary or permanent disability they may suffer as a result of the injury. These laws were originally designed to limit the amount of litigation that ensues from an injury incident by providing standards that employers must follow.

One of those standards is that employers are required to carry workers' compensation insurance. Those who fail to acquire this coverage can have significant financial penalties imposed. In cases where employers have failed to carry legal insurance, there is usually a state sponsored fund to pay benefits to injured workers.

Workers' compensation insurance is generally provided by commercial insurance companies. Several states use a state fund model, and a few have state-owned insurance monopolies.

Simple Do's and Don'ts

- If you are there when accidents occur, make sure employees receive medical care, which could include providing first aid, driving them to your company's workers' comp doctor, or calling 911.
- Do not discourage employees from filing workers' comp claims. If you do, and they go to their own doctor, that will cost your company more. Do not retaliate or punish them in any way for filing a claim. Almost every state prohibits retaliation against employees—including termination, demotion, or pay cut, for filing workers' comp claims.
- Consider whether ADA and/or FMLA apply to the injury. That would entitle workers to additional rights above and beyond workers' comp. For example, if each law entitles them to different amounts of leave, they would be entitled to the longer leave.
- Welcome workers back to work as soon as they are ready. Some supervisors warn employees not to return to work until they are fully recovered. This could violate ADA or your state workers' compensation law.
- Consider light duty. To keep injured employees productive and reduce workers' comp costs, many employers offer light-duty work to employees with work-related injuries.

Retaliation

It is illegal in most states for an employer to retaliate against employees who have filed claims under workers' compensation. Employees cannot be fired for filing a claim nor can they be denied future employment because of a history of having filed a previous claim. As a manager, you must treat all workers' compensation claims seriously, because to not do so could multiply the size of payments by potentially increasing the severity of an injury that has been left unaddressed. Further, employees could take legal action against the organization if they can demonstrate negligence on the part of the employer for dismissing the injury claims.

Fraud

It is equally illegal for workers to falsify workers' compensation claims. Employers have been known to hire private detectives to monitor the activities of someone who is claiming to be disabled as a result of a workplace injury. Doubts about the veracity of a claim may compel an employer to contest the payment of benefits to employees they believe to be committing this type of insurance fraud. Because fraud is typically considered a felony, criminal charges can be made against employees who falsify workers' compensation claims.

Fraud takes many forms and is not exclusively committed by employees or employers. Attorney fraud can result when a lawyer knowingly represents a client who is making a false claim. Health care provider fraud occurs when a medical facility knowingly submits a falsified health care claim under workers' compensation. Even insurance carriers commit fraud when they accept gifts or payments from doctor's offices in exchange for them referring patients making a claim to that specific doctor.

Workplace Hazards

Safety issues can be obvious when the work environment includes hazards such as toxic chemicals, heavy machinery, or construction equipment. If this sounds like your workplace, you and your employees already use certain safety procedures. You operate machinery carefully, you wear special equipment when handling chemicals, etc.

There are other types of hazards not as easy to spot, whether on a factory floor or in an office. Here are some common hazards that may go unnoticed until it is too late:

Computer + employee + chair = carpal tunnel syndrome: If your employees work at computers, you have the potential for carpal tunnel syndrome. The good news is that carpal tunnel is largely preventable. But your company still must pay for injured workers' time off and treatment. Be on the lookout for employees hunched over keyboards or tapping away positions that appear uncomfortable. Other repetitive motions also can produce carpal tunnel, so if employees complains about a sore back, shoulder or wrist, take it seriously.

Driving on company business: Many supervisors consider driver safety only in regard to employees who regularly drive as part of their jobs. There is more to it than that. Do your employees ever drive on company business—to a meeting across town, perhaps? Do you know if they talk on their cell phones while driving? Do they ever consume alcohol at lunch then drive back to the office? Companies will drug test and screen the driving records of employees expected to be behind the wheel regularly, yet they frequently take no precautions regarding occasional drivers. If you know some of your employees are careless drivers, do not let them drive on company business. Arrange a substitute. Be specific about alcohol and drug use while on company business outside the office. Remind employees that cell phone use while driving is dangerous and if you have a policy against it, remind them of that as well.

It is in the air: This refers to such issues as mold, chemicals, cigarette smoke and other inhaled hazards. For some employees, even strong perfume can cause a severe reaction. Buildings with indoor air quality problems are common. The US Environmental Protection Agency estimates that up to 35 percent of workers in ventilated buildings suffer health problems—asthma, many types of respiratory illnesses, lung cancer, Legionnaire's disease, even heart disease—caused by indoor air quality. If your workplace includes chemicals, make sure they are used according to their labeling and applicable regulations of the Occupational Safety and Health Administration (OSHA).

Heavy lifting: Employees moving desks or carrying heavy boxes can strain backs and knock themselves out of commission. If they are not accustomed to heavy lifting, the risk is even greater.

Slip-ups: Wet stairs or an icy parking lot can be a hazard. Identify any slip hazards and make them safer. If the person who falls is not employees, workers' comp does not apply. However, normal personal injury rules do. That could mean a lawsuit and a substantial judgment against your company.

Employees in harm's way: Employers are liable if they put their employees in danger of physical assault. This can occur in several ways. If your workplace is located in a high-crime area, requiring employees to work late could subject them to attack as they leave the building. You also endanger employees, customers, and visitors as well if you know that an employee shows signs of being violent yet do nothing about it.

Nothing Personal

Some supervisors are offended when confronted with workers' comp claims, as if it were a personal indictment. But workers' comp claims are similar to claims made on a health insurance policy. Do not view workers' compensation claims as anything other than what they are—employees exercising their rights.

It is true that a large volume of claims can increase the rates your company pays to its workers' comp insurance carrier. Remember, though, that as a supervisor, you can see to it that workers are treated early for problems. That keeps the claim amount lower in most cases. Should employees seek treatment at emergency rooms of their choice, your company probably will pay more than it would for a workers' comp claim for the same condition.

Strange as it seems, the workers' comp system saves money for employers. That is because workers give up their right to sue their employer for such injuries or illnesses in most cases, regardless of who is at fault in causing the injury. Without workers' comp, every injured employee could sue the company for multimillion-dollar settlements. The legal fees alone would be staggering.

Prepare Now for a Workplace Accident

If you plan your "emergency drill" now, you will be well positioned to respond to accidents or injuries when they occur. You also should know your company's accident procedures so you will be able to answer these questions:

- Who needs to be notified of the accident?
- Are employees permitted to transport injured colleagues to the hospital?
- If the injury is not life threatening, are employees allowed to see their own doctor, or must they see a doctor from a specific list?
- Do you have a defibrillator machine on site and if so, where is it?
- Who in the company knows CPR?

What to Do When an Accident Happens

In the event of an accident there are number of things to be done by either you or in collaboration with your company safety officer. The following should be addressed:

- Administer first aid—and call 911 for a serious injury. Make sure you know your company's procedures for injuries. Where is the first-aid kit? Which employees know CPR?
- If injured employees can do so without further injury, have them reenact what happened. Record your observations of the reenactment as soon as possible.
- Unless employees are incapacitated, fill out a First Report of Injury right away. You also need this kind of report for non-traumatic injuries, such as carpal tunnel and mold exposure, as soon as employees report them to you.
- Get statements from all witnesses and from anyone who spoke to employees just prior to and after the accident. Record those statements immediately—authorities view such statements as

more reliable if a supervisor does not wait days to write them down.

- Inspect the work area and any equipment involved. Are there chairs askew, phones off the hook, supplies knocked off desks? Take pictures. If a cell phone camera is all you have, use that.
- Consider immediate drug tests for injured employees. Generally, employers are allowed to drug test after a work-related injury. However, be careful how you use the results; workers' comp laws in some states may prohibit use of a positive test result as grounds for dismissal.
- Consider whether employees violated company policy or safety regulations. If so, decide if you need to write a corrective action for any violations. Take into account whether the violation was serious, the policy was clear and whether you have routinely cited other employees for the same kind of conduct. Focus on your policies and ignore the potential for a workers' comp claim.
- Make sure to fill out all paperwork. If the injury is serious, employees might require surgery and could be out for weeks under the Family and Medical Leave Act (FMLA). Ask your HR department about running FMLA leave and workers' comp simultaneously. Some states allow it, others do not.
- In any reports or statements, avoid language that could be taken out of context and appear as retaliation for filing a workers' comp claim. For example, pointing out the cost of treating the injury could look like retaliation.
- If the accident involved any machinery or equipment, check all maintenance and service records. Pay particular attention to recent repairs as well as any observations about improper operation of the machinery or equipment.
- Keep in touch with employees if they are out on workers' comp or FMLA leave. Employees who feel forgotten about often have a harder time returning to work.
- Figure out what you can do to prevent any recurrence. Consult with your employees as part of this review.
- Evaluate whether employees will be able to perform the essential functions of their job when they return. If there is doubt, or if

doctors rule it out, talk with HR about offering the employees light duty and other assistance the company can provide. Getting them back to work, even on light duty, can save the company money.

Keeping Accidents from Becoming Lawsuits

Accidents can lead to lawsuits—especially when proper procedures are not followed. Here are seven simple rules to keep accidents from mushrooming into something worse:

Rule #1: Do not retaliate against employees for filing workers' comp claims. Retaliation is illegal in almost every state. Plus, retaliation claims can cost you and your company a great deal. Retaliation means more than firing employees; it also can include changing employee work shifts or job duties, or transferring employees to another location. Any action you take that would make the average employee hesitate to file a workers' comp claim probably is retaliation.

Rule #2: Discipline consistently for safety violations. If your unit has a history of employees violating safety rules without receiving any warnings or write-ups, you may not be able, after someone breaks a safety rule and causes an injury, to fire that employee. At the very least, your effort to fire employees will look like retaliation.

Rule #3: When you discipline, do not make it about the workers' comp claim. When you write up employees for violating a rule, keep the report to that. If your report says, "Employee should have lifted the box with the legs and did not," that is fine. If you add, "and this action also caused a workers' comp claim that is going to cost us over $50,000," you are providing a road map for a retaliation claim.

Rule #4: Make complaining about safety issues easy. You want to be able to stop small safety problems from becoming giant accidents. To know about those problems, your employees must feel confident they will not be berated or ignored for notifying you about them. If employees complain, stop what you are doing and listen; if that is not possible, schedule a time for the conversation. Do not do or say anything to give the impression that only whiners and troublemakers raise safety concerns.

Rule #5: Be mindful of FMLA. Employees are entitled to twelve weeks a year of unpaid FMLA leave. Injured employees may very well be covered by both workers' comp and FMLA. The deciding factor is whether a serious health condition exists. If FMLA applies, make sure either you or the employees immediately designate the leave as FMLA. Rarely can you wait two weeks after an accident to designate FMLA. You can, though, designate FMLA at the beginning of a leave, then follow up with medical certification.

Rule #6: Leave sleuthing to the pros. If you suspect workers of faking or exaggerating injuries to avoid work or get more benefits, do not follow them around with a video camera. Report your concerns to HR, and let them deal with it. The last thing you want is to be in front of a judge on trespassing charges.

Rule #7: Keep in touch with employees on leave. Call them every week or so. They will appreciate the attention and you can use the opportunity to make sure they are getting the help they need. Such regular contact goes a long way to preventing lawsuits. Remember, injured employees have little to do except ponder why they are home and hurting. If they feel no one at work cares about them, bitter feelings can simmer—and boil over into a lawsuit. Talk to them about how much they are missed and what, if any, accommodations they might need to come back part-time. The sooner they return in some capacity, the sooner they will be ready to resume full-time status.

---

[1] "Manager." *The American Heritage® Dictionary of the English Language*, 4th ed. Boston: Houghton Mifflin, 2000. www.bartleby.com/61/. July 2007

[2] Bennis, W. and Goldsmith, J. Learning To Lead: A Workbook On Becoming A Leader. Nicholas Brealey Publishing, 1997.

[3] Mascarenhas, B., Baveja, A. and Jamil, M. "Dynamics of Core Competencies in Leading Multinational Companies", *California Management Review*, vol 40, no. 4, pp. 117-132, 1998.

[4] Merriam Webster Online © 2007-2008 Merriam-Webster Incorporated

[5] See Chapter 5 on Delegation

[6] This lesson presumes that the reader has at least fundamental skills in using office productivity tools such as PowerPoint and does not attempt to teach the mechanical basics of such aids.

[7] segue. (n.d.). *Dictionary.com Unabridged (v 1.1)*. Retrieved November 12, 2007, from Dictionary.com website: http://dictionary.reference.com/browse/segue

www.ingramcontent.com/pod-product-compliance
Lightning Source LLC
Chambersburg PA
CBHW051701170526
45167CB00002B/493